miette

miette

recipes from san francisco's most charming pastry shop

by Meg Ray with Leslie Jonath

photographs by Frankie Frankeny

CHRONICLE BOOKS

SAN FRANCISCO

Text and illustrations copyright © 2011 by Meg Ray.
Photographs copyright © 2011 by Frankie Frankeny.
All rights reserved. No part of this book may be reproduced in
any form without written permission from the publisher.

Library of Congress Cataloging-in-Publication Data available.
ISBN 978-0-8118-7504-2
:
Manufactured in China

Designed by Sara Schneider
Type styling by Janis Reed
Produced by PiperKeller LLC

Miette is a registered trademark of Miette Cakes, LLC.

10 9 8 7 6 5 4 3 2

Chronicle Books LLC
680 Second Street
San Francisco, California 94107
www.chroniclebooks.com

acknowledgments

Mostly, I would like to thank Christopher Ray, my husband of many wonderful years—so many of them devoted to Miette. We spent countless late hours and early mornings in the bakery, hauling things, fixing things, even baking things, and then doing it all over again. And all while raising our daughter Scout, growing his career as a designer and woodworker, and embracing all the sweet struggles of a young family. Chris designed and built the Ferry Building and Hayes Valley shops on a shoestring and tons of hard work. These shops perfectly reflect his gentle character, craftsmanship, and ingenuity.

Infinite gratitude goes to Nancy Kajiyama, the force behind every product at Miette and whose perfectionism is seen on the pages of this book. She tested each recipe for accuracy and made sure the directions are clear and concise. In the near-decade she has been with Miette, her palate is infallible and her patience and kindness have managed the bakery gracefully through thick and thin (mostly thin). She has been a friend, confidant, and, quite literally, my North Star.

Thank you to Caitlin Williams Freeman, whose contributions to Miette are immeasurable. She started as an intern and was brought into the company as a partner within the first year. Together, we ran the business through the exciting early times, filled with recipe development, trips to Europe, and ridiculous amounts of hard work. Her creativity and dedication shaped Miette into what it is today. In writing this book, I recalled many happy memories: listening to the Decemberists at 4:00 A.M., laughing in Amsterdam, and eating box after box of pastries in hotel rooms and trains. Thank you!

From 4:00 A.M. onward and everyday, thank you to all the Miette bakers, unrivaled in their skill and sense of beauty. Special thanks to Sabrina Belara, whose immediate knack for pastry made her an overnight wonder child in the bakery, for decorating most of the cakes photographed in this book. And thank you to all the well-heeled and charming Shop Girls who know our customers as friends and package each box with a perfect bow. And to all our customers who invite us into their lives through their celebrations and all the other days that require cake.

Thank you to Leslie Jonath for an enduring friendship cultivated during the hours of writing this manuscript; for the asparagus and egg salads; for the pho. To Frankie, whose beautiful photography has propelled Miette into so many exciting places, especially this book. And to Bill LeBlond, Sarah Billingsley, Sara Schneider, Doug Ogan, Ben Kasman, Peter Perez, David Hawk, and the rest of Chronicle Books for making this such a beautiful book.

Thank you to Susan Acheson who corrected my French and gave us "miette," and for her lovely Web design work. And to Samuel Leshnick, for his immaculate print and packaging design.

To Michele and Chris Meany, who procured Miette out of the farmers' market for the Ferry Building and their authentic belief in all that they do. And who, with the ironclad fortification of Kathleen Byrne, were there for me when I needed to send in the cavalry. Thank you so much.

To Christina Besher, who shared so much knowledge, hard work, and appreciation of handmade things; everyone at The Food Mill for generously providing us with our first and forever favorite bakery; Peggy and Sue at Cowgirl Creamery for giving me credit when we all knew better; Nigel at Eatwell Farms for his fields of lavender; the guys at Prather Meat for providing much-needed protein and sense of camaraderie; Vanessa Gates, whose handwriting marks the vestige of time; Dexter and Lulu at CUESA for not towing the delivery van; Jane and Zach at the Ferry Building for running the show; the Berkeley Farmers' Market for my first stall and the springboard for everything after that; Alice Waters for her tap on the shoulder and all the doors it opens; Rose Levy Beranbaum as a huge source of inspiration and the surreal delight it was to finally meet her; to ALL the bakers, decorators, and shopgirls at Miette who are forever woven into the character and personality of Miette.

contents

INTRODUCTION

As a young girl, I loved to read my mother's cookbooks. My favorite was the *Better Homes and Garden Cookbook*, the classic 1953 edition, outfitted as it was in its cheerful, tailored gingham cover; and within, fabulous photos of everything befitting a mid-century table. This comforting, simple, homey-but-vibrant aesthetic became my ideal.

It was the 1970s and we moved from Palo Alto, California, to Whidbey Island, near Seattle, Washington. Our house on the island sat among thousands of acres of blackberries, leading to pies, cobblers, and crumbles. My mother worked at a health food store, and brought home a variety of ingredients in bulk, including whole-wheat flour and much-loathed carob chips. Although I was inundated with whole grains, my heart lay in fancy pastries. I found my passion in baking cakes and set out to make the ones I'd seen in my *Better Homes and Gardens Cookbook*. I started at the beginning and baked everything in it.

Initially, I just wanted to frost my cakes and pipe buttercream decorations. I saw baking as the necessary distance to cover before I could pick up the offset spatula and pastry bag. But then I fell in love with the process of baking itself. I began to study the techniques; I taught myself baking through endless trial and error, which produced in turn endless little triumphs and big failures, and vice versa. I made pound cakes, bundts, chiffons, and sponges. Each summer I would enter my cakes in the local county fair. One year, my chocolate cake won the blue ribbon.

I never considered a career in baking. I studied art and design, and somehow wound up working in technology. Baking maintained its allure, and remained the focus of my travels—especially in Paris, where I discovered not only a world of exquisite pastries, but also a charming culture of packaging and presentation. For the French, presentation is as important as the pastry itself and each pastry is entitled to its own special box, wrapped in delicate papers and tied with string. Without realizing it, I was gathering the knowledge to open my own bakery.

the first shop

I started Miette in 2001, during the months leading to the dot-com bust. When I made the transition, I had little idea what I was getting myself into, but I did have a succinct vision: I wanted to create the cakes I had loved as a child and the pastries I had discovered in my travels. *Miette* is the French word for "crumb," which is also a baker's term for describing the texture of a cake—and in scale, it was perfectly fitted to the size of my first shop, a pastel-pink tent at the Berkeley Farmers' Market. For two years, I was easily spotted under the only pastel-pink tent ever to be pitched at the market.

I arranged the tables of the Miette stall with flowers and vintage cake stands, attempting to re-create the splendors of a patisserie amidst the chaotic hustle and bustle of an unpredictable seasonal market. At first, I sold only layer cakes in standard pink bakery boxes. Eventually the product line grew to include pound cakes, cookies, and bars, meticulously wrapped in cellophane and pink paper bags printed with what had quickly become our emblem: a pink rose. From the beginning, Miette's aesthetic was classic and streamlined, feminine but not too girlish, decidedly American but also European, infused with a dreamy, nostalgic quality.

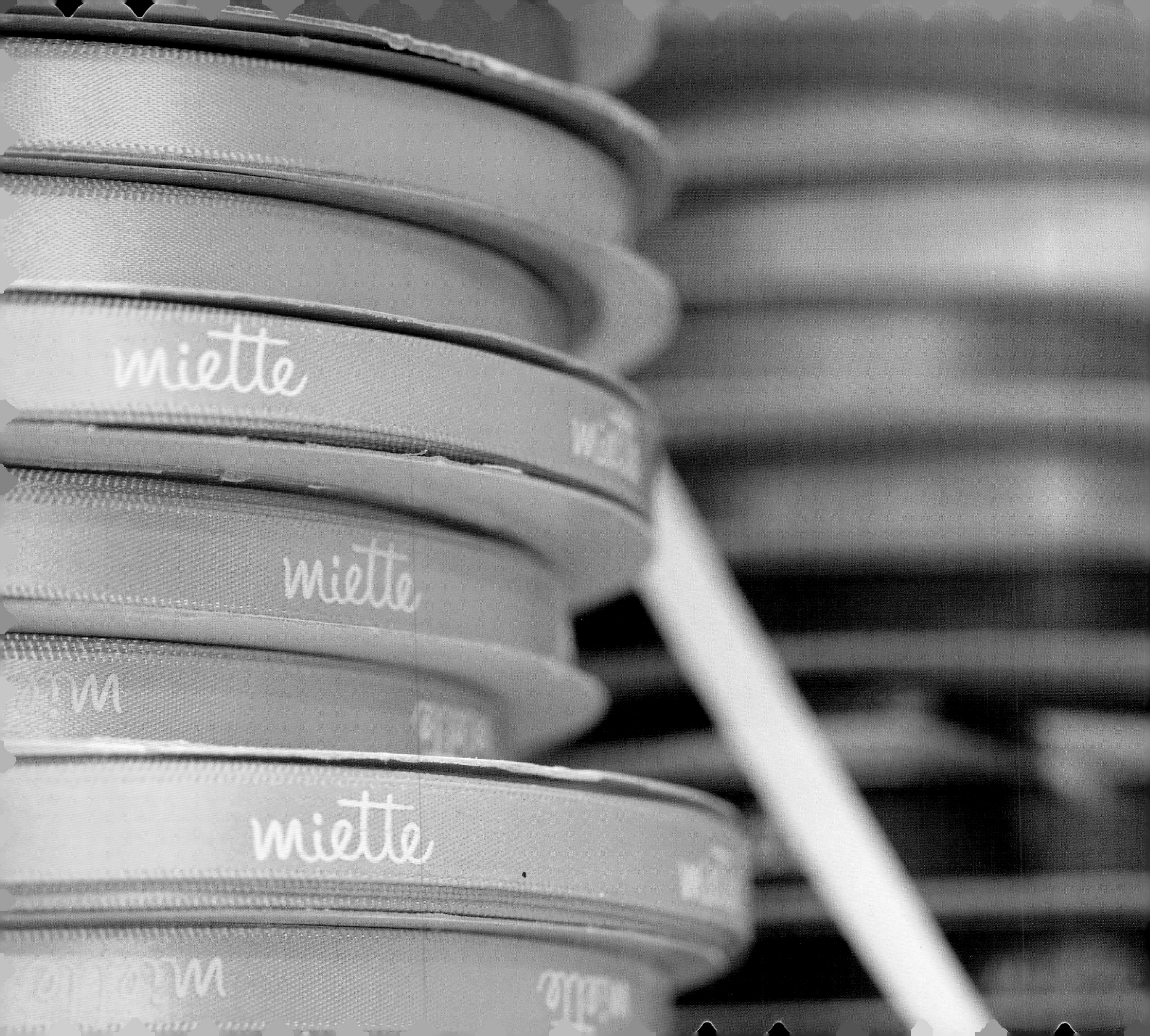
miette
miette
miette

In 2003, we opened our first store in San Francisco's Ferry Building. My husband, Chris, designed the shop (and later our store on Octavia Street) with elaborate crown moldings and vibrant floral wallpaper to create the perfect theater for our cakes and pastries. Today, the shelves are filled with vintage cake plates, jars of brilliant candies, and little vignettes of seasonal themes and narratives. Everything is beautifully packaged in paper, cellophane, string, and colorful satin ribbons. The effect is breathtaking.

american cakes reinvented

Miette started with a passion for cakes, and cakes are still the mainstay of the bakery. Despite the French name, Miette cakes have always been traditionally American, holding at their center the image of the classic American layer cake— a cake that, to my mind, portrays pure happiness. Many of our cakes are finished with a big pink candied rose, a distinction befitting their modern femininity.

With this image in mind, I have been baking my way to the purest versions of these "simple" American classics, with the same criteria for clarity influencing the development of our Lemon Debutantes, Princesses, Tomboys, and all the other sweets on our shelves. While many bakers aspire to make fancy cakes with many fillings and glazes, my aim has always been to create simple cakes that allow you to taste their true flavors. I have no desire to build beyond the point of delicious. Complexity and architecture do not interest me in food, especially not in desserts. I think dessert should look delicious, not impressive. To me, there is nothing more sumptuous than a simple buttery pound cake in which you can actually taste the full-butter flavor.

To complement our cakes, our pastry case is filled with cupcakes, tarts, pots de crème, brownies, shortbreads, and a number of American and French cookie classics. The celebrated Parisian version of the macaron, a centuries-old French meringue-based cookie, was new to me when I tasted one at the venerable Ladurée, but the moment it crumbled with a bit of resistance between my teeth and then melted on my tongue, there was no doubt that this indescribable delicacy had to be added to our repertoire.

small scale

The first thing you may notice about Miette cakes is that they are small. There are two primary reasons for this, one personal and one practical. The first, simply, is that I'm fond of small things. The second is that the nature of the product itself suggested a diminutive size. The plain economics are, making a 9-inch organic cake costs twice as much as the same cake at 6 inches, and a 6-inch cake is an elegant sufficiency, just like a small cookie that is rich and buttery. I carry this sense of proportion through everything we do at the bakery, from creating bite-size cookies and individually portioned custards to choosing pan sizes and keeping decoration simple. Thus we adopted the principle of less is more, also taking a page from the Japanese: Small is better, balance is everything.

Along the same lines, if you stand in front of the pastry cases at Miette, you might think our pastries are numerous and complicated, but in reality, we have streamlined our process to a few perfect recipes. Working from just a core platform of bases and a short list of distinctive fillings, we turn out the entire family of cakes that are the foundation of

our bakery. I believe you are not a better baker by inventing more and more cakes, you are a better baker by doing a few cakes really well. That is the credo that guides what we do at Miette.

local and organic

Also key to our philosophy is the use of the very best ingredients, which we define as local, sustainable, and, whenever possible, organic. From the beginning, this has been a zealous belief of mine; at the same time, I wanted to challenge the stereotype of coarse, earthy "hippy" organic baking, as I was equally as passionate about being in the business of creating light, tender, and elegant cakes and pastries to rival the best pastry kitchens in Europe or America.

My commitment to using unrefined ingredients meant revising a bit of standard fine pastry technique, which emphasizes or even insists on the use of extensively refined ingredients, and led us to evolve at Miette the proportions and techniques you find in this book. In every recipe, the ingredients are meant to shine through. Instead of shortening, which is flavorless, I use real, full-fat, full-flavor butter from Straus Family Creamery; I use organic cane sugars, and flours from local mills (see Sources, page 218). That said, the recipes were tested with the conventional ingredients you are likely to have in your pantry and/or are accustomed to buying and working with, to make sure they would still yield results like those in Miette's kitchens. To achieve a truly Miette product, we recommend you use organic ingredients, especially organic sugar, which is referred to as organic cane sugar.

We also bake in season, selecting the flavors and fillings to use according to the produce the farmers bring to the market each day. One of the main reasons we opened our first shop in the San Francisco Ferry Building, home to one of the premier farmers' markets in the United States, was to have abundant access to the finest fruits and vegetables you have ever seen.

in this book

At Miette, we make our pastries with individual care and attention to detail. Some of the recipes, such as the layer cakes with several components, may be time consuming or challenging for the home baker. We do not sugarcoat the importance of certain steps or techniques, but we have done our best to simplify the methods without compromising what we do in the bakery. Collected here are the recipes for our most beloved pastries, with a particular emphasis on our signature cakes, organized in the same way we think about them at the bakery. Also included are chapters featuring our more casual afternoon cakes; tarts; cookies, bars, and pastries; and candies and creams. A section of essential and versatile recipes at the back covers fillings and frostings, syrups, curds, and mousses—every flourish and all the building blocks necessary to make the recipes in this book, and any of which may serve you in countless baking adventures beyond these covers.

I have never worked in a large-scale kitchen, so everything I know I learned from trial and error, by reading myriad cookbooks, and from the contributions of the amazing bakers who shared their knowledge with me in the Miette kitchen. The recipes in this book are the result of years of experiments and experience, and incorporate the lessons I learned from my many mistakes, so I can anticipate yours. Because this is a bakery book, not a general baking book, we took the approach of embodying most of such accumulated wisdom in the recipes themselves rather than trying to write a comprehensive techniques section. It is often said that baking is an exact science, but for me, baking is enormously creative. Once you know the basic rules, there is room for more than a bit of verve. This is the spirit in which I founded Miette, and I hope that you find that same spirit in the pages of this book.

cakes

Hot Milk Cake
26

Old-Fashioned Cake
59

Lemon Debutante Cake
29

Bittersweet Ganache Cake
63

Princess Cake
34

Tomboy Cake
66

Coconut Mousse Cake
41

Chocolate Chiffon Cake
72

Strawberry Charlotte
45

Bûche de Noël
74

Butter Cake
48

Yellow Cupcakes
77

Bumblebee Cake
51

Cheesecake
79

Double Chocolate Cake
55

CAKES

When I design a cake, I look for uncomplicated flavors that can be assembled in a simple fashion. Primarily American layer cakes, Miette cakes are at once nostalgic and modern, taking you back in time with familiar flavors while exhibiting a refined aesthetic. Most of our cake recipes are familiar classics honed by the principles that define Miette: use of organic ingredients, precision in methodology, and an intentional small scale.

Scale, in particular, is central to the Miette philosophy. All of the cakes in our bakery are made in 6-inch pans, as I believe that most occasions call for no more. When I see a 9-inch cake in another bakery, I find it alarmingly big. If you are going to make a true Miette cake, a 6-by-3-inch round pan is essential. We scaled the master recipes in this chapter to yield two 6-inch cakes, so each time you bake, you will end up with an extra base. While this means you'll need to buy two pans, it makes for a trade-off of convenience, giving you a second foundation cake to work with another time and enough batter to make a 9-inch cake (plus a few cupcakes). All of the base cakes keep well; wrap tightly in plastic and refrigerate for up to 3 days or freeze for up to 2 months.

Miette cakes have minimal decoration, adhering to a simplicity that both belies and underscores their iconic quality. Through the refinement of elements, we have returned the cakes to their original ideals: The Bumblebee is the quintessential birthday cake; the Tomboy is a deconstructed version of chocolate cake with vanilla frosting; and the Lemon Debutante is a diminutive wedding cake. Though the cakes are always pretty, they are never frilly; their beauty comes in the anticipation of wanting to eat them. Cupcakes are cheerfully American, and accordingly, most of these cakes appear in our pastry case in cupcake versions.

The motto of simplicity extends to the Miette baking methodology and in turn, the organization of the chapter of cakes that follows. In this book, as at the bakery, we feature four essential "base" cakes as the foundation for all of the elaborated cakes. Following each base cake recipe are recipes for the constructed cakes, including assembly instructions and, for some, the respective cupcakes, all of which call on an assortment of sumptuous frostings and fillings found at the back of the book. Although each component is relatively simple, the construction and timing can be more complicated, so to repeat, it is important to read through the recipe first to make sure that you understand the whole process. The Coconut Mousse Cake, for example, involves four separate components that require a total of 2 days to make and assemble into the cake.

Finally, at Miette, temperature is everything—not just of the ingredients before you begin, but also in how you serve the cake. Buttercreams are best at room temperature, and therefore need to be removed from the refrigerator at least 4 hours before serving. By contrast, the mousse cakes need to be well chilled and left in the refrigerator until just before you serve them. Each recipe includes information on how the cake should be served for optimal enjoyment.

CAKE-BAKING ESSENTIALS

Baking a perfect cake requires using perfect techniques. While we've integrated the details of Miette techniques into the recipes throughout this book, use the following section for a summary and general reference.

before you begin

Using the right equipment is crucial to your cake-baking success. If you are getting ready to try your hand at the art of cakes for the first time, I strongly recommend you start by reading through the section called "Essential Ingredients" on page 210.

Next, make sure your kitchen is stocked with the following equipment: a heavy-duty stand mixer with paddle and whisk attachments, a microwave oven, medium- and fine-mesh sieves, a bain-marie or double boiler, several heat-resistant rubber spatulas, an instant-read thermometer, cake and loaf pans, a revolving cake stand for decorating, a supply of disposable cardboard cake boards, an offset (icing) spatula, pastry bags and piping tips, and a spackle blade. To create and decorate a Miette cake, a revolving stand is completely essential. Not only will you use it to frost, you will also use it to level and split the layers of the cake.

pan preparation

Cakes require special care with pan preparation, including a coating of both fat and flour (or cocoa powder) that helps the cake fall from the pan easily after baking. For greasing, barely melted butter is best; soften room-temperature butter just a bit further—5 to 10 seconds—in the microwave. Use a pastry brush to coat the pan on all sides and to poke the butter into every nook and cranny. Sprinkle in about ¼ cup (1 ounce) flour and tilt, shake, rotate, and tap the pan to spread the flour in an even coat that covers the bottom, the corners, and all the sides. Whack it upside down, hard, on the countertop to tap out the excess flour; if you tap out onto parchment paper, you can funnel the excess back into your flour bag. When preparing a pan for chocolate cake, use sifted cocoa powder instead of flour—flour may leave an unappealing white residue on the sides of your cake. When using cocoa, sift it beforehand for a smooth patina.

taking the temperature

Paying attention to proper temperature is one of the most important factors in the science of baking, and perhaps most essential for cakes. Mixing ingredients that are the same temperature makes them emulsify more successfully, and you'll see an appreciative difference in the texture of your cake. Start by bringing your butter and eggs to room temperature. Elements that are first heated or cooked must be allowed to cool, while elements that have been in the refrigerator may need to come up to room temperature. Use a thermometer to check the temperature of ingredients when specified, and plan ahead to allow for any necessary waiting periods.

paddle or whisk?

The mixing steps in each recipe call for a specific attachment. The paddle attachment beats and incorporates, while a whisk will add air and generate volume, so the call depends on the nature of the mixture or batter itself. Some ingredients need to be folded gently by hand using a rubber spatula, to avoid deflating an extra-sensitive batter (see page 20).

adding the eggs

Add the eggs to your batters slowly and carefully. This process simply cannot be rushed, as you are emulsifying a liquid into a fat. If not done gradually, you risk "breaking" the batter, the term for when the fat and liquid that are beginning to hold together in a mixture suddenly separate again. Add one egg at a time and make sure that each egg is fully incorporated before adding the next.

mix lightly

As most cakes are highly prone to overmixing, when you reach the step where you add the dry ingredients to the wet ingredients, it is very important to mix lightly. This is because your dough or batter will become tough if you work it to the point that the gluten in the flour starts to form. When making bread, this is the goal of kneading; the opposite is true in baking pastry, where the goal is to develop as little gluten as possible. Once the liquid and flour mixture are combined in the bowl, you need to work with a light touch and alacrity to finish the mixing. While we often do a swift mix in the mixer just until the dry ingredients have been incorporated, I suggest that you always mix by hand after the dry ingredients have been added, using a gently folding motion with a rubber spatula or bowl scraper.

know your oven

Be sure to preheat your oven thoroughly, and fit it with an accurate oven thermometer to ensure a consistent temperature. Learn to think in terms of getting to know your oven—even record observations in your kitchen notes—as understanding where its hot spots are or any other quirks. Position a rack in the center of the oven and arrange the cake pans on the rack so that they do not touch—the heat of the oven must be able to circulate evenly around the pans on all sides. Don't peek! You spent a lot of time and care getting just the right amount of air into the cake so that

the batter is a beautiful network ready to expand, with the application of heat, into tiny combs of air pockets. Opening the oven door during this process may cause the temperature to drop before the structure has solidified, causing the cake to collapse. Resist!

doneness

The most frequently asked question in my cooking classes is, "How long do I bake it?" And I always answer: "Until it's done." This is because every oven and pan, and even different geographic locations, can command a slightly different baking time. It's more important to recognize the signs for doneness. For cakes, you want the top to spring back, a wooden skewer or cake tester to come out clean when inserted into the middle of the cake, and the edges to pull away from the sides. This is simply because you need to know if the middle of the cake is cooked, not just the top or edges. For cookies and tart shells, color is the best indicator, and I take mine to a dark golden color because in my estimation, the flavor quadruples during the last 5 minutes of baking. Also there is a moment when your pastry has that perfect "done" aroma. It takes a fair amount of practice, but with experience, you'll learn to know by smell when things are done.

cooling and depanning

Proper cooling and graceful depanning is the precursor to making the decorating of a cake much easier. The presence of a single jagged edge can foil your finish, because it kicks up crumbs that will inevitably get into the frosting. The first step is to wait for the cake to cool—if it is too warm, it will break apart—but not completely. When there is still a touch of warmth, the cake will slide out of the pan more easily. One means to recognizing the moment is the temperature of the pan: It should be warm, but cool enough to hold comfortably in your hands. To remove the cake, slide the short side of an offset spatula between the edges of the cake and the pan. (An offset blade is better than a knife because it is slightly flexible and has no serration.) Once the blade is inserted, use gentle pressure to maintain a constant connection to the side of the pan, and keep the blade flat and the angle of the spatula straight up and down. You do not want to cut into the cake. Once you have circled the cake, turn the pan upside down and rap an edge of the pan on the counter. The cake should fall out into your hand. Invert the cake right-side up on a wire rack to cool for another hour. A cold cake is easier to cut. So, if time permits, wrap the cake tightly in plastic wrap and put in the refrigerator for 2 hours. The cake will keep, wrapped in plastic, in the refrigerator for up to 3 days. For longer storage, wrap the cake in a second layer of plastic and freeze for up to 2 months.

CAKE ASSEMBLY AND DECORATING BASICS

At Miette, while our cakes look simple, they are very hard to master, as they require expert skill in a few basic techniques. Each recipe walks you through every step and all the keys and cues for the pertinent techniques; the following section takes an opportunity to gather all the details for reference and review, in the form of our standard procedure for assembling and frosting a basic three-layer cake.

Not every cake goes through every step following, and there are variations on the themes (for example, a layer cake with a frosted top but unfrosted sides), but the rundown provides a map to guide you through the last stages of any cake.

leveling the cake
Usually the top of a cake becomes slightly rounded during baking. Since the orientation is reversed for the final cake, in order to use the perfectly smooth side from the bottom of the pan as the top, the dome needs to be removed to make sure the cake stands perfectly straight, a process we simply call "leveling."

A revolving cake stand (often including a nonslip pad) will give you an enormous advantage when trying to make clean cuts, both when leveling and layering a cake. Working on a turntable allows you to turn the uncut width of the cake into the blade of your knife as you go, and so you are less likely to lose your way and slide into a wobbly thickness.

To level a cake, center it on a revolving cake stand. Using a large (longer than the diameter of the cake) serrated knife, press the serrated side of the blade against the surface of the cake at the outside edge, holding the blade perfectly horizontal. Using your other hand, rotate the stand gradually to bring the cake toward you while you saw gently with the knife. Continue sawing while rotating the stand to help your progress until you have passed the knife over the entire top and have removed any curve, creating a perfectly flat and level surface. Stop occasionally as you go and check the surface of the cake at eye level to monitor your progress. Be sure the knife blade stays exactly parallel to the work surface.

splitting the cake into layers

To split the cake into layers, leave it on the rotating cake stand and again take up the serrated knife. To make three equal layers, get eye level with the side of the cake and make small marks with the blade of the knife at spots one-third and two-thirds of the way up from the base. (You can also use a ruler to ensure even layers.) Still working from eye level, cut the first layer: Hold the knife perfectly horizontal and saw gently from edge to edge while rotating the cake toward you, until you have a clean cut all the way through. Pick up the layer and tap it gently to loosen excess crumbs, then brush it as free of all crumbs as you can. Set aside in a clean area of the work surface. Repeat to cut the second layer. The top layer of the base cake becomes the bottom layer of the assembled cake; the bottom layer of the base cake becomes the top of the assembled cake.

stacking the cake

When the cake is leveled and the layers are cut and the frosting and any other fillings are made, you are ready to stack the cake.

Double-check the layers for any remaining crumbs. Tap any crumbs from the revolving cake stand and brush the work surface clean. Place a nonslip pad or damp paper towel on the stand (this will prevent the cake board from slipping while you work) and center a cake board on top. Set aside the original bottom of the cake, with a perfectly flat side from the pan bottom, to be the top of the final cake. Take the original top of the cake, which you leveled, to be the bottom layer of the assembled cake. Center the first layer with its flattest side facing up on the board.

Place a scoop of frosting on top (ice-cream scoops work well). For a 6-inch cake, if you are using a buttercream or cream cheese frosting, you will need ¼ to ½ cup. If using a chocolate ganache, use a ¼ cup or less.

Using an offset spatula, spread the icing to the edges until the layer is fully covered. Gently take up the second cake layer and center it on top of the first, aligning it as precisely as possible. Top with a scoop of the frosting and spread as before. Top with the final layer, flat-side up.

applying the crumb coat

The crumb coat is an initial layer of frosting—a primer coat, just as in painting—that you apply to the cake to hold in the crumbs and mask any minor flaws in the smoothness of the surface before you spread on the presentation layer of frosting. Don't look for beauty in this step. The goal is to contain the crumbs and set down a foundation for perfectly straight sides, a flat top, and a beautiful final coat.

To add the crumb coat, using the offset spatula, apply a scoop of frosting on one side of the cake. Holding the spatula vertically, rotate the cake stand in one direction to spread the frosting evenly around the sides, about ⅛ inch thick. As you work your way around the circumference of the cake, add more frosting as needed to achieve a thin, even primer coat, but do not backtrack or you may pull crumbs back on top of the frosting instead of enveloping them within. Again, the crumb coat will not look finished—what is most important with this step is making sure the layers are aligned perfectly straight up and down on all sides, and are crumb free and smooth. If you have any adjustments to make to align the layers, now is the time to nudge them into position.

As you frost the sides, push the frosting up over the top edge of the cake to make sure the coverage is complete, then use this excess to crumb-coat the top, using the spatula to pull the frosting across the cake toward the center. There should be enough extra frosting from the sides to cover the top, but if necessary, add another small scoop and spread smooth to coat. Transfer the cake on its board to the refrigerator and chill until the crumb coat has hardened and the layers are firmly attached (the crumb coat also protects against sliding), 30 minutes to 1 hour.

reheating and remixing the frosting

When the assembled cake is set and ready for the final coat, remix the frosting, warming slightly if necessary: Place the remaining frosting in a microwave-safe bowl and microwave on high for 15-second intervals, stirring in between each, until the frosting is soft and spreadable. Depending on how long ago the frosting was made and the temperature of the room, this can take from 15 to 30 seconds. If the frosting was frozen it may take up to 2 minutes. (If you overheat the frosting and it melts into liquid, don't panic—just put it back in the refrigerator until it firms up again, about 20 minutes.) If you don't have a microwave, you can also reheat your frosting in a bain-marie or double boiler (see page 215). With this method, you need to transfer the frosting to a heatproof bowl if it's not already in one. Place the bowl over gently simmering water. Stir often, pulling the frosting in from the sides of the bowl as it melts, until soft and smooth throughout, 1 to 2 minutes.

Transfer the warmed frosting to a clean bowl of a stand mixer and fit the mixer with the paddle attachment. Beat at low speed until the frosting is smooth and very shiny, 1 to 2 minutes. Do not use a whisk and do not beat at too high a speed or for too long—any of these will add too much air and produce bubbles that will make the presentation layer look porous and pockmarked.

the presentation layer

To apply the final presentation layer of frosting, transfer the cake from the refrigerator back to the revolving cake stand. Using the offset spatula, apply a scoop of the remixed frosting on one side and, again keeping the spatula in front of you, rotate the cake stand to spread the frosting in a smooth coat, ¼ to ½ inch thick. Continue to add frosting to the sides of the cake, smoothing with the spatula as you make your way around it.

For extra-smooth sides, using a 4-inch spackle blade (see page 217), go around the frosted sides of the cake again, holding the edge of the blade perfectly straight up and down. As always, let the rotation of the stand do the work.

To finish the top, returning to the offset spatula, pull the excess frosting up and over the edges and across the top toward the center, as you did with the crumb coat, working evenly around the cake. Finally, add a small scoop of frosting to the top center of the cake and, holding the spatula flat in the center, rotate the cake stand gradually, moving the spatula to the edges in widening circles while applying gentle pressure to make a smooth, level top coat. If you are going to add piping around the perimeter, you don't need to worry about the seam at the rim being pristine, because the piping will cover it. If you are not adding piping, as in the case of the Bumblebee Cake, push the extra frosting back toward the center, rotating the spatula inward to create a small spiral. Return the cake to the refrigerator and let set until firm, about 30 minutes.

piping and using a pastry bag
To properly use a pastry bag, make a cuff by pulling the top half of the bag down over your hand. Using a rubber spatula, scoop frosting into the bag and pack lightly until the bag is half full. Pull up the cuff and twist it to seal and tighten the frosting down into the cone. Purge the bag of air bubbles by squeezing until there is a burst of air and frosting sputters out of the bag. Keep the bag tightly twisted as you work so that the frosting doesn't push back up onto your hands. If you are piping a ring (for the inner layer that seals the cake layers), hold the bag at a 90-degree angle about an inch over the cake and let the frosting drop as you turn the cake stand and make your way around the cake.

HOT MILK CAKE

makes two 6-inch cakes

Hot Milk Cake is a wonderfully delicate and moist cake that we use in place of a traditional "white" cake. This recipe yields two beautiful 6-inch layers for building on and decorating, and is the foundation for the Lemon Debutante Cake (page 29), the Princess Cake (page 34), the Coconut Mousse Cake (page 41), and the Strawberry Charlotte (page 45).

(Note: You only need one Hot Milk Cake for each of the assembled cakes.)

I originally found the comfortingly named "hot milk cake" in a collection of old New England recipes and have been using it ever since. Milk and butter give it a tender crumb with a sturdy texture and, unlike many traditional white cakes, which often can be dry, this hot milk cake is moist and flavorful. Hot milk cake is technically a sponge cake made with the addition of baking powder and a large amount of butter. The texture is stronger than most sponges—it stands up beautifully to buttercream—but still light and airy enough to absorb a syrup, without becoming gummy or grainy. That means you can flavor it in many different directions or serve it

ingredients

1⅓ CUPS (6½ OUNCES) ALL-PURPOSE FLOUR

2 TEASPOONS BAKING POWDER

¼ TEASPOON KOSHER SALT

½ CUP (4 OUNCES) UNSALTED BUTTER, AT ROOM TEMPERATURE

½ CUP WHOLE MILK

1½ CUPS (10½ OUNCES) SUGAR

3 LARGE EGGS

½ TEASPOON VANILLA EXTRACT

preparation

1. Read through or review the "Cake-Baking Essentials" section beginning on page 18.

2. Liberally butter two 6-by-3-inch cake pans and dust with flour (see page 19). Tap out the excess flour.

3. Preheat the oven to 350 degrees F.

4. Sift together the flour, baking powder, and salt into a bowl and set aside.

5. In a saucepan over medium-low heat, combine the butter and milk and heat, stirring occasionally, until the butter is melted, 3 to 4 minutes. (Alternatively, in a microwave-safe bowl, combine the butter and milk and microwave on high at 10-second intervals, stirring between each, until the butter is melted.) Pour the milk mixture into a large bowl. Set aside and let cool to slightly above room temperature; an instant-read thermometer should register between 80 and 85 degrees F. You want the milk and butter to remain incorporated, so whisk the mixture occasionally and vigorously while it is cooling and up until you add it to the batter.

on its own with berries and whipped cream. Hot milk cake is often used as the base for wedding cakes.

This is a challenging cake, in that there are a couple of steps you need to manage simultaneously. The key to success lies completely in temperature control, so it is crucial that you have an instant-read thermometer at the ready. Two separate mixtures that started hot are combined only when they have cooled to the same room temperature. Using a thermometer will help ensure the proper emulsification of the subtly special batter.

6. In the top pan of a double boiler or in a bowl for a bain-marie, whisk together the sugar, eggs, and vanilla. Fit the top pan or bowl over (but not touching) simmering water in the bottom pan or a saucepan and gently warm the mixture, stirring, just until the sugar is dissolved and the thermometer registers 110 degrees F, about 10 minutes. Pour the egg mixture through a medium-mesh sieve into the bowl of a stand mixer. Fit the mixer with the whisk attachment and whisk on high speed until the mixture is light and fluffy and has cooled to slightly above room temperature (between 80 and 85 degrees F), about 10 minutes. (Note: The batter becomes more stable as the mixture cools; this is an important factor in creating a cake with good structure.)

7. Stop the mixer. Add the sifted dry ingredients and mix on low until just incorporated. The batter should be smooth. Check the milk mixture to make sure it is fully cooled, then slowly pour it into the batter, whisking on low speed. Stop mixing as soon as the batter is well blended and smooth. Remove the bowl from the mixer, scrape down the sides of the bowl again, and fold by hand a few times with the spatula. Divide the batter between the prepared pans. Bake until the cakes are golden brown and a tester inserted in the center comes out clean, 30 to 35 minutes.

8. Transfer to wire racks and let cool in the pans for about 20 minutes. When the cakes are cooled enough to handle the pans but still a tad warm to the touch, carefully run an offset spatula around the edges of the pans to loosen them, then invert the cakes onto the racks and remove the pans. Let cool for about 30 minutes longer. Wrap the cakes tightly in plastic wrap and refrigerate to ensure that the interiors are completely cooled before decorating, at least 1 hour or for up to 3 days. To freeze, wrap tightly in a second layer of plastic wrap and store in the freezer for up to 2 months.

LEMON DEBUTANTE CAKE

makes one 6-inch layer cake

If it could be said that any of our cakes went to finishing school, it would be this one. With a perfectly smooth gown of frosting and delicate piping, this cake is our most turned out; thus we call it the Debutante. It has three layers of sponge cake infused with tart lemon syrup, filled with lemon curd, frosted with light lemony buttercream and is finished with scalloped piping and a sugar flower. The Lemon Debutante Cake takes the Hot Milk Cake in a direction that fully maximizes its capability. The cake absorbs the syrup and holds up the curds and cream without becoming overwhelmed. Here is a textbook example of how to build a layer cake; think of it as a kind of cake compulsory, akin to skating in perfect circles. The decorating techniques for this cake are exactly the same as those you need to make a wedding cake.

This recipe calls for both a Lemon Buttercream made with Lemon Curd and for additional Lemon Curd, so plan to make the Lemon Curd first and give it ample time to chill before making the Lemon Buttercream.

ingredients

1 HOT MILK CAKE (PAGE 26)

¼ CUP LEMON SIMPLE SYRUP (PAGE 207)

ABOUT 3 CUPS LEMON BUTTERCREAM (PAGE 186)

ABOUT 4 TABLESPOONS LEMON CURD, CHILLED (PAGE 200)

1 SMALL CANDIED SUGAR FLOWER (SEE SOURCES, PAGE 218)

preparation

1. Read through or review the "Cake Assembly and Decorating Basics" section beginning on page 21.

2. Make the Hot Milk Cake as directed and make sure it is cool inside and out. (If frozen, let thaw in the refrigerator, 3 to 4 hours. If time demands, you can thaw on the countertop, 1 to 2 hours, but be careful not to let it sit for too much longer before you begin working with it, as a cold cake is easier to cut.

3. Clear a space in the refrigerator large enough for the cake on a cake board (see page 215). If making the simple syrup, let cool to room temperature. If you made the buttercream previously, remix the frosting until spreadable (see page 23).

4. Set a revolving cake stand on a clean, dry work surface and place the cake, top-side up, on the stand. Using a serrated knife and holding the blade perfectly horizontal, remove any dome from the top of the cake to level it. While you saw gently with the knife, use your other hand to rotate the stand gradually and bring the cake toward you. Get eye level with the cake as needed to make sure you are holding the knife exactly level. Repeat to split the cake into three equal layers.

continued

5. Arrange all three cake layers on the work surface. Using your hands, tap off and brush away excess crumbs. Reserve the original bottom layer (flat-dark-side, or pan-side, up) to be the top layer of the assembled cake. Tap any crumbs off the cake stand as well, and brush the work surface clean. Using a pastry brush, brush the top of each layer with an ample amount of the lemon syrup.

6. Place a nonslip pad or damp paper towel on the cake stand to prevent slipping and center a cake board on top. Take up the original top of the cake, which you leveled, to be the bottom layer of the assembled cake. Center the first layer of cake with its flattest side facing up on the board.

7. Fit a pastry bag with a medium (½- or ⅝-inch) round tip and fill halfway with the buttercream. Pull up the cuff and twist it to seal and tighten the frosting down into the cone. Purge the bag of air bubbles by squeezing the bag until there is a burst of air and frosting sputters out of the bag. Keep the bag tightly twisted so that the frosting doesn't come back up on your hands. Holding the bag upright at a 90-degree angle, pipe a ring of buttercream about ½ inch in diameter around the outer edge of the cake to create a barrier. Spoon about 2 tablespoons of the curd onto the center of the cake and, using an offset spatula, spread it smoothly all over the top of the cake, out to the edges of the frosting barrier. Take up the filled pastry bag again and, starting at the inside edge of the barrier and working inward, pipe a tight spiral of buttercream over the curd. Gently smooth the buttercream with the offset spatula. You now have a frosted layer laced and dotted with pockets of lemon curd.

8. Arrange the second cake layer on top and press down lightly to seal and secure. Repeat to frost with the buttercream and curd as above. Place the reserved top piece, flat-side (crust-side) up, on top. You are now ready to apply the crumb coat.

9. Using the offset spatula, apply a scoop of frosting on one side of the cake. Holding the spatula vertically more or less in front of you, rotate the cake stand in one direction to spread the frosting evenly around the sides, about ⅛ inch thick. As you work your way around the circumference of

continued

STEP 4a: Using a serrated knife, remove any dome to level the cake.

STEP 4b: Hold the knife level and split the cake into three equal layers.

STEP 7a: Starting at the inside edge of the frosting barrier, pipe a tight spiral inward.

STEP 7b: Gently smooth the buttercream with an offset spatula.

the cake, add more frosting as needed to achieve a thin, even primer coat, but do not backtrack or you may pull crumbs back on top of the frosting instead of enveloping them within. The crumb coat doesn't need to look finished; just make sure the sides are straight. Nudge the layers into position if needed. As you frost the sides, push the frosting up over the top edge of the cake to make sure the coverage is complete, then use this excess to crumb-coat the top, using the spatula to pull the frosting across the cake toward the center. There should be enough extra frosting from the sides to cover the top, but if necessary, add another small scoop and spread smooth to coat.

10. Place the cake, on the cake board, in the refrigerator until the crumb coat has hardened and the layers are firmly attached, 30 minutes to 1 hour. Cover and refrigerate the remaining buttercream (you should have about 1½ cups).

11. When you are ready to finish frosting, remix the remaining buttercream: Place in a microwave-safe bowl and microwave on high for 30-second intervals, stirring in between each, until the frosting is soft, smooth, and spreadable, without any lumps, 15 seconds to 1 minute. If you don't have a microwave, you can also reheat the frosting in a bain-marie or double boiler. With this method, place the frosting in a heatproof bowl or the top pan of a double boiler. Place the bowl over (but not touching) gently simmering water in a saucepan or the bottom pan of a double boiler. Stir often, pulling the frosting in from the sides of the bowl as it melts, until soft and smooth throughout, 1 to 2 minutes.

12. Transfer the frosting to a clean bowl of a stand mixer and fit the mixer with the paddle attachment. Beat at low speed just until the frosting is smooth and very shiny, 1 to 2 minutes. Do not use a whisk and do not beat at too high a speed or for too long—any of these will add too much air and produce bubbles that will make the presentation layer look porous and pockmarked.

13. When the crumb coat is set, transfer the cake on its board from the refrigerator back onto the revolving cake stand, with the nonslip pad or a damp paper towel underneath. Add the presentation layer of

buttercream: Using the offset spatula, apply a scoop of the remixed frosting on one side of the cake and, again keeping the spatula in front of you, rotate the cake stand to spread the frosting in a smooth coat, ¼ to ½ inch thick. Continue to add frosting to the sides of the cake, smoothing with the spatula as you make your way around it.

14. For extra-smooth sides, using a 4-inch spackle blade (see page 217), go around the frosted sides of the cake again, holding the edge of the blade perfectly straight up and down. Let the rotation of the stand do the work.

15. To finish the top, pull the excess frosting up and over the edges and across the top toward the center, as you did with the crumb coat, working evenly around the cake. Finally, still using the offset spatula, add a small scoop of buttercream to the center of the cake and, holding the spatula flat in the center of the cake, rotate the cake stand clockwise, moving the spatula to the edges in gradually widening circles while applying gentle pressure to make a smooth, even coat. Since you are going to add piping around the perimeter, you don't need to worry about the seam at the rim being pristine. Return the cake to the refrigerator and let set until firm, about 30 minutes.

16. To decorate the cake, pipe a small shell border: Fit a pastry bag with a small (¼- or ⅜-inch) star tip and fill halfway with the remaining butter-cream. Pointing the tip at the top rim of the cake at a 45-degree angle, apply a small burst of pressure to create a tiny hump and release, moving up just a tad to make a shell shape; repeat this motion around the perim-eter to create the shell border. Refill the bag; holding it at a 45-degree angle at the base of the cake, use the same motion to pipe the bottom border. Place the candied sugar flower in the center of the cake. Very carefully transfer the cake on the board to a presentation platter or plate.

17. This cake needs to be served at room temperature. Serve at once, or hold at room temperature for up to 4 hours. For longer storage, refrigerate for up to 2 days and remove from the refrigerator 4 hours before serving.

PRINCESS CAKE

makes one 6-inch layer cake

This cake arrived with her title and it is aptly deserved, as there is something regal in the lovely dome shape and pale green color. Originally made in the 1930s for the three princesses of Sweden, Miette's version is strictly traditional—almost. We added a modern ingredient and a contemporary aesthetic: white chocolate fondant instead of marzipan (and a tint that is a bare whisper of green). We love the smooth silky feel and sophisticated look of the fondant, and at holiday time, we turn this cake into a snowball by keeping the fondant white and covering it with shiny white sugar. At Easter, we use three different colors to tint the fondant, filling our case with a pastel array of cakes.

When I teach this cake in my classes, the students can hardly wait to roll out the fondant. But this step must be saved for the end, when the cake has been tucked away in the refrigerator and all the crumbs are cleared away. When working with fondant, your work surface must be pristine and your hands must be clean. Also note, the raspberry jam for this cake needs to be thick and seedless.

continued

ingredients

1 HOT MILK CAKE (PAGE 26)

¼ CUP RASPBERRY SIMPLE SYRUP (PAGE 207)

ABOUT ¼ CUP PASTRY CREAM (PAGE 202), FULLY CHILLED

3 TABLESPOONS SEEDLESS RASPBERRY JAM, WARMED UNTIL POURABLE

2 CUPS HEAVY CREAM

4 TABLESPOONS POWDERED SUGAR

1 POUND WHITE CHOCOLATE FONDANT (SEE SOURCES, PAGE 218)

3 DROPS GREEN FOOD COLORING (OPTIONAL)

1 DROP YELLOW FOOD COLORING (OPTIONAL)

CORNSTARCH FOR ROLLING

1 CANDIED ROSE AND LEAF (OPTIONAL; SEE SOURCES, PAGE 218)

20 INCHES MOSS-GREEN SATIN RIBBON, 1 INCH WIDE

1 DECORATIVE STRAIGHT PIN

preparation

1. Read through or review the "Cake Assembly and Decorating Basics" section beginning on page 21.

2. Make the Hot Milk Cake as directed and make sure it is cool inside and out. (If frozen, let thaw in the refrigerator, 3 to 4 hours. If time demands, you can thaw on the countertop, 1 to 2 hours, but be careful not to let it sit too much longer before you begin working with it, as a cold cake is easier to cut.

3. Clear a space in the refrigerator large enough for the cake on a cake board (see page 215). If making the simple syrup now, let cool to room temperature.

continued

A loose jam will disappear into the layers, and seeds are an annoyance when paired with the other creamy textures.

This cake is famously complicated and may take days to make, depending on your stamina and how each of the components comes together. I don't recommend you start with this cake; perhaps think of it as a potential goal once you have completed your other cakes. This will be your crowning achievement.

4. Set a revolving cake stand on a clean, dry work surface and place the cake, top-side up, on the stand. Using a serrated knife and holding the blade perfectly horizontal, remove any dome from the top of the cake to level it. While you saw gently with the knife, use your other hand to rotate the stand gradually and bring the cake toward you. Get eye level to the cake as needed to make sure you are holding the knife exactly level. Repeat twice to split the cake into three equal layers. Set one of the layers aside for snacking.

5. Arrange the two cake layers on the work surface. Using your hands, tap off and brush away excess crumbs. Turn the original bottom layer flat-dark-side, or pan-side, up; reserve this to be the top layer of the assembled cake. Tap any crumbs off the cake stand as well, and brush the work surface clean. Using a pastry brush, brush the top of each layer with an ample amount of the raspberry syrup.

6. Place a nonslip pad or damp paper towel on the cake stand to prevent slipping and center a cake board on top. Take up the original top of the cake, which you leveled, to be the bottom layer of the assembled cake. Center the first layer of cake with its flattest side facing up on the board.

7. Fit a pastry bag with a small (¼- or ⅜-inch) round tip and fill halfway with the pastry cream. Pull up the cuff and twist it to seal and tighten the pastry cream down into the cone. Purge the bag of air bubbles by squeezing the bag until there is a burst of air and pastry cream sputters out of the bag. Keep the bag tightly twisted so that the frosting doesn't come back up on your hands. Holding the bag at a 90-degree angle, pipe a ring of pastry cream about ¼ inch in diameter around the outer edge of the cake to create a barrier. Spoon the strained raspberry jam onto the center of the cake and, using an offset spatula, spread it smoothly all over the top of the cake, up to the edges of the pastry cream barrier. Take up the filled pastry bag again and, starting at the inside edge of the barrier and working inward, pipe a tight spiral over the jam using the remaining pastry cream. Using an offset spatula, gently smooth the inside of the spiral. Place the reserved top piece, flat-side up, on top and press down lightly to seal and secure.

continued

STEP 8a: Shape the whipped cream into a dome about 3 inches high.

STEP 8b: Mold the dome to the edges of the cake, rotating the turntable while holding the spatula to even the curve.

STEP 10a: Carefully drape the fondant.

STEP 10b: Adhere the fondant to the shape of the cake.

STEP 10c: Trim the base of the fondant, leaving a ¼-inch overhang.

STEP 10d: Lift the edge of the cake with an offset spatula and begin tucking the fondant under it.

STEP 10e: Continue tucking all of the fondant. Smooth the cake surface.

STEP 11:   Wrap the ribbon around the base of the cake.

8. In a chilled bowl, using an electric mixer set on high speed, whip together the heavy cream and powdered sugar until stiff peaks form. It is very important to make sure that the whipped cream is firm enough, or the cake will slump. Scoop the firmly whipped cream carefully onto the top of the cake and shape it into a dome about 3 inches high, mounding it all the way to the edges, rotating the turntable while holding the offset spatula to even the curve. Place the cake, on the cake board, in the refrigerator while you prepare the fondant.

9. On a clean work surface, and using clean hands, knead the fondant until soft and pliable. If you want the cake's "dress" to have a delicate green tint, add the green and yellow food coloring, a tiny drop at a time, until the fondant reaches the color you desire. Dust the surface of the fondant and a rolling pin with cornstarch. Occasionally lift and rotate the fondant so that it does not stick to the table. Roll the fondant out into a circle about 10 inches in diameter and ¼ inch thick. Using a clean, soft-bristled pastry brush, brush away any visible cornstarch.

10. Transfer the cake on its board from the refrigerator back onto the revolving cake stand, with the nonslip pad or a damp paper towel underneath, and set it near the fondant. Very carefully lift the fondant circle over the backs of your forearms. Center the fondant over the dome of whipped cream and then slowly drape it over the mound of cream and sides of the cake, sweeping your forearms away when you reach the board. Use your palms to smooth and pat the fondant gently to help it adhere to the shape of the cake all around. Using the tip of a sharp knife or a pizza wheel, trim the base of the fondant, leaving an overhang of about ¼ inch around the base of the cake. Lift one edge of the cake with an offset spatula, and very carefully tuck a small section of the fondant underneath the cake. Repeat all around the cake until the entire train of the fondant is neatly tucked under the cake and the surface is smooth all over.

11. Very carefully transfer the cake on the board to a presentation platter. Top with the candied rose and leaf, if desired. Wrap the ribbon neatly around the base of the cake and secure with the straight pin. Serve at once or refrigerate for up to 8 hours. Remove from the refrigerator 30 minutes before serving.

COCONUT MOUSSE CAKE

makes one 6-inch layer cake

The Coconut Mousse Cake is our celebration of winter, with its pure white coconut flakes and the perfect consolation it offers during the season when our fruit choices are limited. Coconut is at once familiar, exotic, and nostalgic; the inspiration for this cake was a tall 1950s-style American layer cake covered in shredded coconut. Miette's version adds a layer of mousse and a coconut syrup that enhances the nutty-sweet coconut flavor.

This cake has many steps and some of the ingredients, particularly the coconut purée for the mousse, can be difficult to track down. See our Sources section (page 218), and give yourself plenty of time to tackle the steps individually. You need to make both the mousse and the icing the same day you assemble the cake. The mousse cake is assembled in a cake pan and needs time in the refrigerator to set. Pipe the boiled icing and add the final decoration several hours before serving. You can make this in either three or four layers. You will need about ¼ cup of mousse per layer.

ingredients

1 HOT MILK CAKE (PAGE 26)

¼ CUP COCONUT SIMPLE SYRUP (PAGE 207)

2 CUPS FRESHLY MADE COCONUT MOUSSE (PAGE 199)

ABOUT 2 CUPS FRESHLY MADE BOILED ICING (PAGE 192)

¾ CUP (2½ OUNCES) SHREDDED DRIED COCONUT

preparation

1. Read through or review the "Cake Assembly and Decorating Basics" section beginning on page 21.

2. Make the Hot Milk Cake as directed and make sure it is cool inside and out. (If frozen, let thaw in the refrigerator, 3 to 4 hours. If time demands, you can thaw on the countertop, 1 to 2 hours, but be careful not let it sit too long before you begin working with it, as a cold cake is easier to cut.)

3. Clear a space in the refrigerator large enough for the cake on a cake board (see page 215). The mousse cake will need several hours to set up.

4. If making the simple syrup now, let cool to room temperature. Make the mousse as directed.

5. Set a revolving cake stand on a clean, dry work surface and place the cake, top-side up, on the stand. Using a serrated knife and holding the blade perfectly horizontal, remove any dome from the top of the cake to level it. While you saw gently with the knife, use your other hand to rotate the stand gradually and bring the cake toward you. Get eye level to the cake as needed to make sure you are holding the knife exactly level. Repeat to split the cake into three or four equal layers.

continued

6. Arrange all the cake layers on the work surface. Using your hands, tap off and brush away excess crumbs. Turn the original bottom layer flat-dark-side, or pan-side, up; reserve this to be the top layer of the assembled cake. Using a pastry brush, brush the top of each layer with an ample amount of the coconut syrup.

7. Line a clean 6-by-3-inch cake pan with plastic wrap, leaving about 3 inches of overhang all around the sides to use later as a handle. Take up the original top of the cake, which you leveled, to be the bottom layer of the assembled cake. Place this first layer, syrup-side up, in the lined pan. Scoop one-third of the mousse on top of the cake layer and use an offset spatula to level it. Top with the second layer of cake, syrup-side up, and press down lightly to seal and secure. Add another layer of mousse. Repeat with the third layer if making a four-layer cake.

8. Place the reserved top piece, flat-dark-side up, on top. Cover with plastic wrap and carefully transfer the cake to the refrigerator. Let set for at least 3 hours and up to 2 days.

9. To unmold the mousse cake, wrap a hot towel around the pan for 1 minute and gently shake to loosen the cake. Invert the pan onto a cake board on a clean work surface, then gently lift off the pan. If it resists, give a little tug on the plastic-wrap "handle." When the pan is off, peel the plastic-wrap lining from the cake. Transfer the cake on its board onto the revolving cake stand, with a nonslip pad or damp paper towel underneath.

10. This cake requires only one coat of icing. Using the offset spatula, apply a generous scoop of the icing on one side of the cake. Keeping the spatula in front of you, rotate the cake stand to spread the icing in a smooth coat about 1 inch thick. (It needs to be thick enough to hide the sides of the cake, but not drooping down the sides.) Add more icing as you go, but do not back track! The icing will be covered with coconut, so it is not important for it to be perfect; however, the coat of icing should be straight up and down on all sides, as well as crumb free and smooth. As you frost the sides, push the icing up over the top edge of the cake to make sure the coverage is complete, then use this excess to frost the top, using the spatula to pull the icing across the cake toward the center. There should be enough icing from the sides to cover the top, but if necessary, add another small scoop.

11. Using a cupped hand, apply the dried coconut to the sides and top of the cake, pressing gently to help it adhere. Very carefully transfer the cake on the board to a presentation platter. Gather up any excess coconut and press it onto the cake, or reserve for another use. Refrigerate the cake for at least 1 hour and up to 8 hours. Remove from the refrigerator 30 minutes before serving.

STRAWBERRY CHARLOTTE

makes one 6-inch layer cake

When we announce the arrival of the Strawberry Charlotte, the cakes are pre-sold before they even make it into the display case. They are magnificent to behold: a powdery band of ladyfingers tied up with a bow and a jumbled crown of tiny strawberries. And the inside is just as remarkable, enriched by a mousse that is as creamy as it is fresh and bright.

Charlottes are a French dessert traditionally made in a mold with ladyfingers and Bavarian cream or mousse. Typically the pan is lined with the ladyfingers and the filling is added. We found this technique to be incredibly difficult. The solution we devised is to mold the mousse separately, and pipe the ladyfinger batter in a way that lets it bake into a connected band of cookies. At assembly time, this allows you to wrap the cookie sash around the cake in one fell swoop.

Mousse is a delightful way to carry the flavor of fresh fruit into a cake, contributing creaminess and swoon-worthy unctuousness at the same time. In the cake, too—a simple, buttery sponge with a touch of syrup

continued

ingredients

1 HOT MILK CAKE (PAGE 26)

¼ CUP RASPBERRY SIMPLE SYRUP (PAGE 207)

ABOUT 2 CUPS FRESHLY MADE STRAWBERRY MOUSSE (PAGE 198)

TWO 3-BY-10-INCH BANDS LADYFINGERS (PAGE 204), TRIMMED TO A TOTAL OF 19 INCHES (SEE NOTE, PAGE 47)

APPROXIMATELY 28 INCHES MOSS-GREEN SATIN RIBBON, 1 INCH WIDE

1 PINT FRESH STRAWBERRIES, PREFERABLY SMALL AND WHOLE WITH STEMS ATTACHED, OR HULLED AND SLICED IF LARGER

1 DECORATIVE STRAIGHT PIN (OPTIONAL)

preparation

1. Read through or review the "Cake Assembly and Decorating Basics" section beginning on page 21.

2. Make the Hot Milk Cake as directed and make sure it is cool inside and out. (If frozen, let thaw in the refrigerator, 3 to 4 hours. If time demands, you can thaw on the countertop, 1 to 2 hours, but be careful not to let it sit too long before you begin working with it, as a cold cake is easier to cut.)

3. Clear a space in the refrigerator large enough for the cake on a cake board (see page 215). The mousse cake will need several hours to set up.

4. If making the simple syrup now, let cool to room temperature. Make the mousse as directed.

continued

for background complexity—there is little to distract you from the fruit. To heighten the color of the mousse, you can add a few raspberries to the fruit juice. Add the ladyfingers and the berries for garnish about 3 hours before serving. We get our strawberries from Swanton Farms, one of the farmers at the Ferry Building market. The berries are small and incredibly flavorful, and sometimes they still have their stems attached, making the charlotte look like a woodland wedding cake.

You will only use two of the three layers of cake in this assembly. At the bakery, the third layer becomes the first in the next cake; but at home you should just enjoy it with your coffee or tea. This cake has many parts and is best tackled over a couple of days, but you should make the strawberry mousse the day you will assemble the cake, as mousse sets up quickly. The mousse recipe makes more than you will need for this cake so we recommend putting it in ramekins or in a bowl to serve separately. (It keeps for 2 days so you don't have to eat everything all at once.)

There are few things that provide as deep a sense of accomplishment in the pastry kitchen as when you tie the bow around this striking cake for the finishing touch.

5. Set a revolving cake stand on a clean, dry work surface and place the cake, top-side up, on the stand. Using a serrated knife and holding the blade perfectly horizontal, remove any dome from the top of the cake to level it. While you saw gently with the knife, use your other hand to rotate the stand gradually and bring the cake toward you. Get eye level to the cake as needed to make sure you are holding the knife exactly level. Repeat to split the cake into three equal layers.

6. Reserve the top layer for another use (see recipe introduction). Arrange the two cake layers on the work surface. Using your hands, tap off and brush away excess crumbs. Tap any crumbs off the cake stand as well, and brush the work surface clean. Using a pastry brush, brush the top of each layer with an ample amount of the raspberry syrup.

7. Line a clean 6-by-3-inch cake pan with plastic wrap, leaving about 3 inches of overhang all around the sides to use later as a handle. Put the bottom layer, syrup-brushed flat-side up, in the pan. Scoop about 1 cup of the mousse on top of the cake layer and use an offset spatula to level it. Top with the second layer of cake, syrup-side down, and press down lightly to seal and secure. Add as much of the remaining mousse as you need to fill the pan to the rim.

8. Very gently place another piece of plastic wrap on top, directly on the surface of the mousse (this prevents a skin from forming). Carefully transfer the cake to the refrigerator and let set for at least 3 hours and up to 2 days.

9. To unmold the mousse cake, wrap a hot towel around the pan for 1 minute and gently shake to loosen the cake. Invert the pan onto a cake board on a clean work surface, then gently lift off the pan. If it resists, give a little tug on the plastic-wrap "handle." When the pan is off, peel the plastic-wrap lining from the cake. Invert the cake again, mousse-side up. Place the cake on a presentation platter.

STEP 7: Add as much of the remaining mousse as you need to fill the pan to the rim.

STEP 10: Carefully secure the ladyfingers around the sides of the cake.

10. One at a time, carefully secure the two bands of connected ladyfingers, powdered-sugar-side out, around the sides of the cake, pressing them into the mousse to secure. Wrap the ribbon around the cake, positioning it about halfway up the sides, and tie it snugly in a knot. Or, trim it to about 22 inches and secure it snugly with the straight pin. Don't allow any slack, because in addition to its pretty form, the ribbon is functioning to bond together the ladyfingers.

11. Refrigerate the cake for at least 2 hours and up to 2 days. Remove from the refrigerator 30 minutes before serving. Just before serving, arrange the strawberries on top in an artful pattern.

note

If the bands of ladyfingers are too tall, measure the overage, place on a cutting board, and cut off the bottom tips to match your measurement. If the combined bands are too long, measure the excess, place on a cutting board, and cut off the excess in a vertical strip to match your measurement, preferably between two cookies.

BUTTER CAKE

makes two 6-inch cakes

Yellow cake can be nondescript, but this butter cake has tons of character. Its texture is like a pound cake, so it holds up beautifully to rich frostings and cuts incredibly well—all told, the perfect layer cake. As with the other base cakes in this chapter, you can make this cake up to 3 days in advance, but here, because the flavor of butter and rich tones of vanilla actually improve with time, we strongly recommend making it at least a day ahead. We use this recipe for our Bumblebee Cake (page 51), where it is layered with chocolate ganache for a truly decadent yellow layer cake. As with the other base cakes, this recipe yields two cakes; the second one stores beautifully, ready for decorating anytime.

The technique for this cake includes creaming the butter and sugar, to create plenty of air bubbles in the batter; note that it is important to take your time with this step, otherwise the cake, loaded with a generous amount of butter, may become overly dense. The more you cream it, the more air bubbles you create, which then expand in the oven, giving the cake a lighter texture—just be sure not to let the butter melt before or

ingredients

1⅔ CUPS (8 OUNCES) ALL-PURPOSE FLOUR

2 TEASPOONS BAKING POWDER

¾ TEASPOON KOSHER SALT

¾ CUP PLUS 2 TABLESPOONS (7 OUNCES) UNSALTED BUTTER, AT ROOM TEMPERATURE

1 CUP (7½ OUNCES) SUGAR

10 LARGE EGG YOLKS, AT ROOM TEMPERATURE

⅔ CUP BUTTERMILK

1 TEASPOON VANILLA EXTRACT

preparation

1. Read through or review the "Cake-Baking Essentials" section beginning on page 18.

2. Liberally butter two 6-by-3-inch cake pans and dust with flour. Tap out the excess flour.

3. Preheat the oven to 350 degrees F.

4. Sift together the flour, baking powder, and salt into a bowl and set aside.

5. In the bowl of a stand mixer fitted with the paddle attachment, combine the butter and sugar and beat on medium speed until light colored and fluffy, 10 to 12 minutes. Add the egg yolks in three additions, beating until completely combined after each, about 2 minutes per addition, and stopping to scrape down the sides of the bowl with a rubber spatula before adding more yolks. Raise the speed to high and beat for 30 seconds to fully combine.

during beating. You must also take your time adding the eggs into the creamed mixture, adding one at a time and beating until completely emulsified, to keep the structure intact. Remember, adding any liquids too quickly can break a batter (see page 19). This cake is too heavy to use as a cupcake so we have provided a separate Yellow Cupcakes recipe (page 77).

Use the best, richest unsalted butter you can find. Ours comes from Straus Family Creamery, which is only 50 miles from our shop. And while the recipe calls for a lot of egg yolks to give it a lovely yellow hue, you can save the extra whites for making Boiled Icing (page 192) or Buttercream (see pages 185–189).

6. In a bowl, stir together the buttermilk and vanilla. With the mixer on low speed, add the sifted dry ingredients in three additions alternately with the buttermilk mixture in two additions, beginning and ending with the dry ingredients. After each addition, beat until just combined. Remove the bowl from the mixer, scrape down the sides of the bowl again, and fold by hand a few times with the spatula.

7. Divide the batter between the prepared pans and smooth the tops. Bake until the cakes are lightly browned and a tester inserted in the center comes out clean, 35 to 40 minutes.

8. Transfer to wire racks and let cool in the pans for about 20 minutes. When the cakes are cooled enough to handle the pans but still a tad warm to the touch, carefully run an offset spatula around the edges of the pans to loosen them, then invert the cakes onto the racks and remove the pans. Let cool for about 20 minutes longer. Wrap the cakes tightly in plastic wrap and refrigerate to ensure that the interiors are completely cooled before decorating, at least 1 hour or for up to 3 days. To freeze, wrap tightly in a second layer of plastic wrap and store in the freezer for up to 2 months.

BUMBLEBEE CAKE

makes one 6-inch layer cake

This cake is named the "Bumblebee" because its cross section, yellow cake striped with bittersweet chocolate ganache, looks like the midsection of a bumblebee. As is the case with the simple Butter Cake, it gets better with time. I actually prefer to eat it on the third day after I make it, as the flavors have time to meld and the butter gets into every crumb. I love it for breakfast. The ganache is easier to spread if you allow it to get very soft.

Assembling this cake is more difficult than it looks because it is very hard to get a perfectly clean edge on the top of the cake. We solve this problem by pulling the extra frosting into a swirl at the center of the cake, which is then adorned and hidden with a sugar rose.

ingredients

1 BUTTER CAKE (PAGE 48)

¼ CUP SIMPLE SYRUP (PAGE 207)

ABOUT 2 CUPS CHOCOLATE GANACHE (PAGE 195)

1 CANDY ROSE (OPTIONAL; SEE SOURCES, PAGE 218)

preparation

1. Read through or review the "Cake Assembly and Decorating Basics" section beginning on page 21.

2. Make the Butter Cake as directed and make sure it is cool inside and out. (If frozen, let thaw in the refrigerator, 3 to 4 hours. If time demands, you can thaw on the countertop, 1 to 2 hours, but be careful not to let it sit too much longer before you begin working with it, as a cold cake is easier to cut.)

3. Clear a space in the refrigerator large enough for the cake on a cake board (see page 215). If making the simple syrup and ganache now, let cool to room temperature.

4. Set a revolving cake stand on a clean, dry work surface and place the cake, top-side up, on the stand. Using a serrated knife and holding the blade perfectly horizontal, remove any dome from the top of the cake to level it. While you saw gently with the knife, use your other hand to rotate the stand gradually and bring the cake toward you. Get eye level to the cake as needed to make sure you are holding the knife exactly level. Repeat to split the cake into four equal layers.

continued

5. Arrange all four cake layers on the work surface. Using your hands, tap off and brush away excess crumbs. Turn the original bottom layer flat-dark-side, or pan-side, up; reserve this to be the top layer of the assembled cake. Tap any crumbs off the cake stand as well, and brush the work surface clean. Using a pastry brush, brush the top of each layer with a conservative amount of the syrup.

6. If the ganache is at room temperature, check the consistency; you may need to add a tablespoon or so of hot water to get the desired spreadable softness. If you made the ganache earlier and it has been chilled to a solid, scoop it into a microwave-safe bowl and microwave on high in 30-second increments. It should be the consistency of room-temperature butter. If it is not yet soft, microwave in 30-second increments until it reaches the desired consistency. Transfer to a mixer fitted with the paddle attachment and beat on medium speed until lightened in color, smooth, and spreadable, 3 to 4 minutes total. You may need to add a tablespoon or so of hot water.

(If you don't have a microwave, you can reheat the ganache in a bain-marie or double boiler. With this method, place the ganache in a heat-proof bowl or the top pan of a double boiler. Place the bowl over, but not touching, gently simmering water in a saucepan or the bottom pan of a double boiler. Stir often, pulling the ganache in from the sides of the bowl as it melts, until soft and smooth throughout, 4 to 5 minutes.)

7. Place a nonslip pad or damp paper towel on the cake stand to prevent slipping and center a cake board on top. Take up the original top of the cake, which you leveled, to be the bottom layer of the assembled cake. Center this first layer of cake with its flattest side facing up on the board.

8. Using an ice-cream scoop or large spoon, scoop about ¼ cup of the ganache onto the cake. Using an offset spatula, smooth the ganache to the edges. Arrange the second cake layer on top and press down lightly to seal and secure. Repeat to frost with the ganache as above. Continue with the third cake layer. Place the reserved original bottom layer, flat-dark-side up, on top. You are now ready to apply the crumb coat.

9. Using the offset spatula, apply a scoop of ganache on one side of the cake. Holding the spatula vertically more or less in front of you, rotate the cake stand in one direction to spread the ganache evenly around the sides, about ⅛ inch thick. As you work your way around the circumference of the cake, add more ganache as needed to achieve a thin, even primer coat, but do not backtrack or you may pull crumbs back on top of the frosting instead of enveloping them within. The crumb coat doesn't need to look finished; just make sure the sides are straight. Nudge the layers into position if needed. As you frost the sides, push the ganache up over the top edge of the cake to make sure the coverage is complete, then use this excess to crumb-coat the top, using the spatula to pull the ganache across the cake toward the center. There should be enough extra ganache from the sides to cover the top, but if necessary, add another small scoop and spread smooth to coat.

10. Place the cake, on the cake board, in the refrigerator until the crumb coat has hardened into a thin crust and the layers are firmly attached, 30 minutes to 1 hour. Cover and refrigerate the remaining ganache alongside.

11. When you are ready to finish frosting, reheat and remix the remaining ganache: Place in a microwave-safe bowl and microwave on high for 30-second intervals, stirring in between each, until the ganache is soft, smooth, and spreadable, without any lumps, 30 seconds to 1 minute. Or, reheat in a bain-marie or double boiler (see Step 6).

12. Transfer the warmed ganache to a clean bowl of a stand mixer fitted with the paddle attachment. Beat at low speed just until the frosting is smooth and very shiny, 1 to 2 minutes. Do not use a whisk and do not beat at too high a speed or for too long—any of these will add too much air and produce bubbles that will make the presentation layer look porous and pockmarked.

continued

13. When the crumb coat is set, transfer the cake from the refrigerator back onto the turntable, with the nonslip pad or a damp paper towel underneath. If a frosting crust has formed on the cake board, gently scrape it off using the offset spatula. Add the presentation layer of ganache: Using the offset spatula, apply a scoop of the warmed and remixed frosting on one side of the cake and, again keeping the spatula in front of you, rotate the cake stand to spread the frosting in a smooth coat, ¼ to ½ inch thick. Continue to add ganache to the sides of the cake, smoothing with the spatula as you make your way around it.

14. For extra-smooth sides, using a 4-inch spackle blade (see page 217), go around the frosted sides of the cake again, holding the edge of the blade perfectly straight up and down. Let the rotation of the stand do the work.

15. To finish the top, pull the excess ganache up and over the edges and across the top toward the center, as you did with the crumb coat, working evenly around the cake. Finally, still using the offset spatula, add a small scoop of ganache to the center of the cake and, holding the spatula flat in the center of the cake, rotate the cake stand clockwise, moving the spatula to the edges in gradually widening circles while applying gentle pressure to make a smooth, even coat. Since you are going to sculpt around the perimeter, you don't need to worry about the seam at the rim being pristine. Return the cake to the refrigerator and let set until firm, about 30 minutes.

16. To sculpt the edging detail, hold an offset spatula against the bottom edge of the cake at a 20-degree angle. Rotate the cake stand a few times. This should create a rough ruffle. Wipe the stand clean of all ganache streaks. Top with the candy rose, if desired.

17. This cake needs to be served at room temperature. Serve at once, or hold at room temperature for up to 4 hours. For longer storage, refrigerate for up to 2 days and remove from the refrigerator 4 hours before serving.

DOUBLE CHOCOLATE CAKE

makes two 6-inch cakes

Made with both melted dark chocolate and cocoa powder, this chocolate cake is rich, complex, and bittersweet—a perfect match for sweet frostings, which is how you'll find it paired in our Tomboy Cake (page 66), Bittersweet Ganache Cake (page 63), and Old-Fashioned Cake (page 59). As with the other base cakes, this recipe yields two 6-inch cakes, so you can have one on hand in your freezer to decorate anytime.

This cake is infallibly moist. Part of the reason for its fine-crumb texture is that we strain the batter through a sieve to remove any lumps before pouring it into the pans. Straining out the lumps rather than trying to stir them into the batter prevents overmixing and leads to a dense cake. We also sift the cocoa before dusting the pans, a technique that will give the exterior finish of your cakes a lovely smooth patina.

For the Old-Fashioned Cake, we bake this cake in a contour pan, a special design with a beveled edge around the bottom that yields an elegant cake with an almost seamless form. Contour pans come in standard sizes, including 6-inch, and are easily found online (see Sources, page 218).

ingredients

1½ CUPS (7½ OUNCES) ALL-PURPOSE FLOUR

1¼ CUPS (4½ OUNCES) NATURAL UNSWEETENED COCOA POWDER (SEE NOTE)

1½ TEASPOONS BAKING SODA

½ TEASPOON BAKING POWDER

¾ TEASPOON KOSHER SALT

2 OUNCES 70 PERCENT CACAO CHOCOLATE, COARSELY CHOPPED

1 CUP BOILING WATER

1 CUP BUTTERMILK

½ TEASPOON VANILLA EXTRACT

2 LARGE EGGS, AT ROOM TEMPERATURE

½ CUP VEGETABLE OIL

2¼ CUPS (15 OUNCES) SUGAR

preparation

1. Read through or review the "Cake-Baking Essentials" section beginning on page 18.

2. Liberally butter two 6-by-3-inch regular or contour cake pans and dust with sifted cocoa powder. Tap out the excess cocoa.

3. Preheat the oven to 350 degrees F.

4. Sift together the flour, cocoa powder, baking soda, baking powder, and salt into a bowl and set aside.

continued

5. Put the chocolate in a heatproof bowl and pour the boiling water over it. Whisk until the chocolate is melted. Let the mixture cool for 15 minutes.

6. In a separate bowl, whisk together the buttermilk and vanilla. Set aside.

7. In the bowl of a stand mixer fitted with the whisk attachment, whisk the eggs on high speed until foamy, about 2 minutes. Reduce the speed to low and slowly pour in the oil, whisking until combined, about 30 seconds. Raise the speed to medium and whisk until fully incorporated, about 30 seconds longer.

8. Reduce the speed to low and slowly pour the cooled chocolate mixture into the egg mixture. Slowly pour in the buttermilk and vanilla mixture. Add the sugar and whisk until the batter is smooth and liquid, about 2 minutes.

9. Stop the mixer. Remove the bowl and add the sifted dry ingredients and mix until just incorporated, preferably by hand, lifting and folding in from the bottom center. Using a rubber spatula, scrape down the sides of the bowl and mix again just briefly by hand. The batter may still look a little lumpy, but stop mixing.

10. Pour the batter through a medium-mesh sieve into a large measuring cup or bowl to remove any lumps. Press against the solids in the sieve with a rubber spatula to push through as much batter as possible, then discard the lumps. Divide the batter between the prepared pans. Bake until the tops spring back when lightly pressed and a tester inserted in the centers comes out clean, about 45 minutes.

11. Transfer to wire racks and let cool in the pans for about 20 minutes. When the cakes are cooled enough to handle the pans but still a tad warm to the touch, carefully run an offset spatula around the edges of the pans to loosen them, then invert the cakes onto the racks and remove the pans. (Note: If you are making the Old-Fashioned Cake and therefore using a contour pan, just invert the pans and drop them sharply onto the racks; they should fall out cleanly. Using an offset spatula in a contour pan will mar the edges of the cake.) Let cool for about

20 minutes longer. Wrap the cakes tightly in plastic wrap and refrigerate to ensure that the interiors are completely cooled before decorating, at least 1 hour or for up to 3 days. To freeze, wrap tightly in a second layer of plastic and store in the freezer up to 2 months.

note

We use natural cocoa powder not Dutch-processed, as the Dutch-processed cocoa has been treated with an alkalizing agent that heightens the color but gives it a milder flavor. For this recipe, it is important to use natural product such as Scharffen Berger to attain a deep, dark chocolate flavor.

DOUBLE CHOCOLATE CUPCAKES

Line two standard muffin tins with paper liners. Fill each cup two-thirds full with batter. Bake at 350 degrees F until the tops spring back and a tester inserted in the center of a cupcake comes out clean, 20 to 25 minutes. Transfer the pans to a wire rack and let cool completely in the pan. Makes about 2 dozen cupcakes.

OLD-FASHIONED CAKE

makes one 6-inch cake

This cake evolved from a desire to bring together our beloved Double Chocolate Cake and Boiled Icing; the dense bittersweet cake is offset deliciously by the soft, marshmallow-like icing. When we first tried to apply the icing to the sides of the cake, however, it just rolled off like a small, sweet avalanche. Our solution was to mound the icing on top like a big puffy cloud; then we topped it with a bright red cherry for a simple stroke of contrast. We named the cake the "Old-Fashioned" because of its beautifully simple American flavors and aesthetic. It is our fastest and easiest cake to make.

To make this cake, you need to bake the chocolate layer cake in a contour pan—a specialty pan with gently sloped sides and round edges at the bottom that produces a cake with a subtle dome shape (see Sources, page 218). The icing must be made the same day that you are going to assemble and serve the cake.

ingredients

1 DOUBLE CHOCOLATE CAKE (PAGE 55) BAKED IN A CONTOUR PAN

ABOUT 1½ CUPS FRESHLY MADE BOILED ICING (PAGE 192)

1 LARGE MARASCHINO CHERRY, WITH STEM INTACT

preparation

1. Read through or review the "Cake Assembly and Decorating Basics" section beginning on page 21.

2. Make the Double Chocolate Cake as directed, and make sure it is cool inside and out. (If frozen, let thaw in the refrigerator, 3 to 4 hours. If time demands, you can thaw on the countertop, 1 to 2 hours, but be careful not to let it sit too much longer before you begin working with it, as the texture will lose quality.)

3. Center the cake on a presentation plate or platter, dome-side up. Clear a space in your refrigerator large enough for the cake on its platter.

4. Fit a pastry bag with a medium (½- or ⅝-inch) round tip and fill halfway with the icing. Pull up the cuff and twist it to seal and tighten the icing down into the cone. Purge the bag of air bubbles by squeezing the bag until there is a burst of air and icing sputters out of the bag. Keep the bag tightly twisted so that the icing doesn't come back up on your hands. Holding the piping tip at a 90-degree angle about 1 inch above the center of the cake, squeeze firmly to release a large mound of icing. Keep the tip slightly submerged in the icing and continue. Begin to slowly squeeze the bag again, more gently this time, so that the icing continues to flow outward (like lava) and move the bag slightly in tiny, smooth, uniform circles to increase the flow until you make a mound

continued

that tops the cake, 2 to 3 inches thick. Stop about ¼ inch from the edge to show off the contour of the cake. When the icing process is complete, pull the tip straight up the center to make a point in the middle for the final flourish.

5. Gently squeeze the maraschino cherry to drain it of any excess syrup, and wrap it in a paper towel for about 10 minutes. This will keep it from bleeding on the icing.

6. Place the cherry in the center of the cake with the stem raised attractively at a 45-degree angle. Serve immediately or refrigerate the cake for up to 8 hours. Remove from the refrigerator 30 minutes before serving. It is best to eat the cake the same day you make it.

OLD-FASHIONED CUPCAKES

To decorate Double Chocolate Cupcakes (page 57) Old-Fashioned style, fit a pastry bag with a medium (½- or ⅝-inch) round tip and fill the bag halfway with icing. Pull up the cuff and twist it to seal and tighten the icing down into the cone. Purge the bag and icing of air bubbles by squeezing the bag until there is a burst of air and icing sputters out of the bag. Starting at the center of a cupcake at a 90-degree angle and about ½ inch from the top, pipe a dollop of icing. To complete, swiftly pull the pastry bag straight up in a snapping action to make a peaked finish. Repeat to frost the remaining cupcakes. Place a decoration, such as a candied Boston baked bean, in the center of each cupcake.

BITTERSWEET GANACHE CAKE

makes one 6-inch cake

This moist, dense chocolate cake, poured over with a bittersweet chocolate ganache, is the best thing you've ever eaten. We pair chocolate with chocolate but with such surprising variation in texture and flavor it never becomes overwhelming.

The glaze on this cake is so glossy it rivals the sheen of patent leather. To get the same finish as we do at Miette, you need an immersion blender—and a bit of practice with glazing. Don't worry about using too much ganache; it's extremely reusable, so you can always reclaim the extra that rolls off the cake. It's better to pour too much than not enough.

Although I have said that I strongly prefer most of our cakes in the 6-inch size, this is one cake that is just as elegant made in a 9-inch pan. I've even made it as large as 14 inches without losing any of its appeal; in fact, it becomes grand. I love to serve it topped with lightly whipped cream or any ice cream.

ingredients

1 DOUBLE CHOCOLATE CAKE (PAGE 55) BAKED IN A COUNTOUR PAN

ABOUT 2 CUPS CHOCOLATE GANACHE (PAGE 195)

20 INCHES BROWN STRIPED SATIN RIBBON, ⅜ INCH WIDE

preparation

1. Read through or review the "Cake Assembly and Decorating Basics" section beginning on page 21.

2. Make the Double Chocolate Cake as directed, and make sure it is cool inside and out. (If frozen, let thaw in the refrigerator, 3 to 4 hours. If time demands, you can thaw on the countertop, 1 to 2 hours, but be careful not to let it sit too much longer before you begin working with it, as the texture will lose quality.)

3. Place the cake on a wire rack set over a rimmed baking sheet or jelly-roll pan. Clear a space in your refrigerator large enough for the cake on the baking sheet.

4. Read this step very carefully, paying special attention to every detail, most of which are designed to prevent air from entering the ganache; it is the most important step for this cake. Scoop the ganache into a microwave-safe bowl. (If the ganache was made earlier and has been chilled to a solid, first microwave on high for 1 minute. Stir very gently so as not to agitate the chocolate, which would introduce air.) Microwave at 10-second intervals, gently stirring between each, until the ganache is mostly liquid. Have ready an immersion blender, which you will use to make the glaze very smooth and pourable. Add about

continued

2 tablespoons very hot water to the ganache, and let the water sit on top. Insert the head of the blender, while it is off, into the ganache very slowly at a 30-degree angle; you do not want to trap any air in the compartment of the head. When the head of the blender is submerged, upright the blender to a 90-degree angle and turn it on. Begin to make gentle circles, never up and down and never breaking the surface, until the chocolate is very shiny and smooth, 3 to 5 minutes. Be patient, as you will need more time than you think. When you begin to see a shine develop, you think you are done, but go on a little longer.

5. Pour the glaze over the cake, beginning at the edges and spiraling to the middle. This helps to ensure an even coat all over the cake. Rap the tray lightly on the table to settle the glaze. Refrigerate until set, about 45 minutes.

6. Repeat the glazing step once more, scraping up the extra ganache from the baking sheet and making sure to repeat the process above to restore the glaze to its shiniest level. Be sure the cake is thoroughly and evenly coated with glaze. Refrigerate as before to set up and harden, approximately 45 minutes. Make sure you let the first layer set thoroughly. If not, the second coat will cause the first to ripple. To transfer the cake to a cake board and then onto the presentation plate or platter, heat the blade of a knife in hot water and carefully go around the outside perimeter of the cake, then insert a large spatula under the cake edge and lift, making sure not to rip the chocolate from the rack before transferring the cake to the cake board and the presentation plate or platter. Use the sharp knife to carefully trim off the excess ganache around the outside perimeter of the cake, wiping down the cake board with the edge of a damp cloth. (Scrape any remaining ganache off the baking sheet and save it for another use.)

7. Wrap the ribbon around the base of the cake, and secure one end to the other with a dot of ganache. Wipe the board clean of all ganache streaks. This cake needs to be served at room temperature. Serve at once, or hold at room temperature for up to 4 hours. For longer storage, refrigerate for up to 2 days and remove from the refrigerator 4 hours before serving.

note

To make a 9-inch cake, prepare a 9-inch contour pan as directed for the 6-inch pan. Pour the Double Chocolate Cake batter into the pan until it comes up to ½ inch from the edge of the pan. (You will have some leftover batter; discard or use for a few Double Chocolate Cupcakes or mini cakes in ramekins.) Bake at 350 degrees F until the top springs back when lightly pressed and a tester inserted in the center comes out clean, 55 to 60 minutes. Assemble as directed, using about 3 cups ganache.

TOMBOY CAKE

makes one 6-inch layer cake

This cake was on its way to becoming a conventionally frosted layer cake when I noticed how unexpectedly voluptuous the bare sides looked with the frosting poking out between the layers. This cake has a gamine quality, a little rough around the edges—a bit of a tomboy with a little rose on top.

The expression "tomboy" has become part of the Miette vocabulary for a particular decorating style; any cake and frosting combination can become a Tomboy. The Double Chocolate Cake is the perfect candidate because its layers are so moist that they do not dry out even when exposed to the air. You'll notice a lot of attention to crumb control in this recipe; to achieve the finished look and keep the buttercream pristine, you need to guard against every fleck.

I especially like the Tomboy's proportion of frosting to cake; just a bit of each per bite, and never too much frosting. Key to the look of this cake is the star tip, used to pipe the frosting borders that give the frosting its slightly frilly edge.

ingredients

1 DOUBLE CHOCOLATE CAKE (PAGE 55)

ABOUT 3 CUPS RASPBERRY BUTTERCREAM (PAGE 187) OR FLAVOR OF YOUR CHOICE

1 ICING ROSE AND SMALL GREEN LEAF (OPTIONAL; SEE SOURCES PAGE 218)

preparation

1. Read through or review the "Cake Assembly and Decorating Basics" section beginning on page 21.

2. Make the Double Chocolate Cake as directed, using a regular cake pan, and make sure it is cool inside and out. (If frozen, let thaw in the refrigerator, 3 to 4 hours. If time demands, you can thaw on the countertop, 1 to 2 hours, but be careful not to let it sit too long before you begin working with it. This cake needs to be scrupulously crumb free, so make sure it is still cold when you begin to work.)

3. Clear a space in the refrigerator large enough for the cake on a cake board (see page 215). If you made the buttercream previously and it has been refrigerated, follow the instructions on page 23 to reheat and remix the frosting.

4. Set a revolving cake stand on a clean, dry work surface and place the cake, top-side up, on the stand. Using a serrated knife and holding the blade perfectly horizontal, cut the cake into three equal layers. While you saw gently with the knife, use your other hand to rotate the stand gradually and bring the cake toward you. Get eye level to the cake as needed to make sure you are holding the knife exactly level. (You do not need to level the top of the cake.)

continued

5. Arrange all three cake layers on the work surface. Using your hands, tap off and brush away excess crumbs. Turn the original bottom layer flat-dark-side, or pan-side, down; reserve this to be the bottom layer of the assembled cake. (This is the reverse of the usual method of using the flat side for the top of a finished cake, but here the smooth edges from the cake pan give a nice finished look to the unfrosted base of the Tomboy.) Tap any crumbs off the cake stand as well, and brush the work surface clean.

6. Place a nonslip pad or damp paper towel on the cake stand to prevent slipping and center a cake board on top. Take up the reserved bottom of the cake and center it on the board, first double-checking it for crumbs and brushing any off or pressing them into the sides.

7. Fit a pastry bag with a medium (½- or ⅝-inch) star tip and fill about halfway with the buttercream. Pull up the cuff and twist it to seal and tighten the frosting down into the cone. Purge the bag of air bubbles by squeezing the bag until there is a burst of air and frosting sputters out of the bag. Keep the bag tightly twisted so that the frosting doesn't come back up on your hands. Holding the bag at a 90-degree angle, pipe a ring of frosting around the outer edge of the cake, keeping a ⅛-inch border at the very edge. Starting at the inner edge of the border, spiral inward filling in the center of the ring to make an even layer of buttercream. Holding an offset spatula flat on the inside ring of frosting, with the spatula centered on the cake, smooth the inside of the ring, leaving the piped edges untouched.

8. Double-check a second cake layer for crumbs, then place it on top of the buttercream layer. Using your fingertips, gently center the cake on top. Be sure not to press too hard so that the buttercream spreads over the edge. Repeat with a layer of buttercream just like you did on top of the first cake layer.

9. Double-check the third and final cake layer for crumbs, then place it on top. Using your fingertips and gentle pressure, press down in the center and out to the edges to coax the frosting to align with the cake edge, but not beyond, on all sides.

STEP 7a: Starting at the inner edge of the frosting border, pipe a spiral of buttercream inward.

STEP 7b: Smooth the inside frosting, leaving the edges untouched.

STEP 10a: For the top layer, pipe a ring of buttercream around the edge, leaving a ⅛-inch margin.

STEP 10b: Fill in the center with slightly more frosting than the inner layers.

10. For the top layer, pipe a ring of buttercream around the edge, leaving a ⅛-inch margin. Fill in the center with slightly more frosting than the inner layers. Using a small offset spatula, smooth the center first by rotating the cake stand, then gradually work out to the edges, pushing the frosting out very slightly as you go.

11. If desired, in the center of the cake, scoop out a little hole in the frosting to make a setting for the rose. Nestle the rose in the hole and arrange the leaf next to it at a 45-degree angle. Very carefully transfer the cake on the board to a presentation platter.

12. This cake needs to be served at room temperature. Serve at once, or hold at room temperature for up to 4 hours. For longer storage, refrigerate for up to 3 days and remove from the refrigerator 4 hours before serving.

CHOCOLATE CUPCAKES

To decorate Double Chocolate Cupcakes (page 57) Tomboy style, fit a pastry bag with a medium (½- or ⅝-inch) star tip and fill the bag halfway with buttercream (see pages 185–189). Purge the bag and frosting of air bubbles by squeezing the bag until there is a burst of air and frosting sputters out of the bag. Starting at the edge of a cupcake at a 90-degree angle and about ½ inch from the top, pipe a rosette of frosting, then continue squeezing while moving the bag in smooth, uniform, concentric circles to make a layer 2 to 3 inches thick almost to the edges of the cupcake. To complete, swiftly pull the pastry bag straight up in a snapping action to make a peaked finish. Repeat to frost the remaining cupcakes. Top cupcakes with sprinkles or with a candied flower and a leaf (see Sources, page 218).

CHOCOLATE CHIFFON CAKE

makes one 11-by-17-inch jelly-roll cake

I think of chiffon cake as the "king of cakes" because it is easy to make—practically infallible—and infinitely versatile. The texture of the cake is fluffy and "downy," like the gossamer fabric it is named for. We use this cake in the Bûche de Noël (page 74).

Made with oil instead of butter, this hybrid between a sponge and a butter cake won't harden when cold, which makes it ideal for pairing with fillings, like mousse, that need to be refrigerated to set up properly. And unlike a sponge cake, the chiffon cake is moist without syrup.

ingredients

¾ CUP (3 OUNCES) ALL-PURPOSE FLOUR

¼ CUP NATURAL UNSWEETENED COCOA POWDER (SEE NOTE, PAGE 57)

½ TEASPOON BAKING POWDER

½ TEASPOON BAKING SODA

⅛ TEASPOON KOSHER SALT

6 EGGS SEPARATED, PLUS 1 WHOLE EGG

⅓ CUP (2½ OUNCES) SUGAR, PLUS ¼ CUP (2 OUNCES)

¼ CUP VEGETABLE OIL

⅛ CUP WATER

1 TEASPOON VANILLA EXTRACT

⅛ TEASPOON CREAM OF TARTAR

preparation

1. Read through or review the "Cake-Baking Essentials" section beginning on page 18.

2. Liberally butter the bottom of an 11-by-17-inch jelly-roll pan and fit the bottom with parchment paper. Do not grease the sides of the pan.

3. Preheat the oven to 350 degrees F.

4. Sift together the flour, cocoa powder, baking powder, baking soda, and salt into a bowl and set aside.

5. In the bowl of a stand mixer fitted with the whisk attachment, combine the egg yolks, whole egg, and the ⅓ cup sugar and whisk on high speed until light colored and ribbony, about 5 minutes. Drizzle in the oil slowly and whisk until fully combined.

6. In a measuring cup, stir together the water and vanilla. With the mixer on low speed, pour the liquid into the batter in a thin stream. Whisk until very smooth, about 3 minutes.

7. With the mixer still on low speed, add the sifted dry ingredients in three additions, beating until just combined after each addition. Do not over-mix. Remove the bowl from the mixer and transfer the batter to another bowl. Set aside.

8. Combine the egg whites and cream of tartar in a clean bowl. Using the stand mixer or an electric mixer fitted with the whisk beaters, whisk the whites on medium speed until foamy, 1 to 2 minutes. Slowly add the remaining ¼ cup sugar and continue to whisk until medium-stiff peaks form. Using a rubber spatula, fold the whites into the batter in three additions, until no streaks remain. Coax the batter very gently into the prepared pan and gently smooth the top with the spatula. Bake until the cake springs back when touched, 30 to 35 minutes.

9. Transfer the jelly-roll pan to a wire rack and let cool. With a serrated knife, cut the perimeter of the cake. Lift the cake by picking up the corner edges of the parchment and moving the cake to a clean work surface. (For the Bûche de Noël, leave the parchment paper on the cake.) If not using the cake immediately, tightly wrap the cake and pan in plastic wrap and store in the refrigerator for up to 2 days or in the freezer for up to 2 months.

BÛCHE DE NOËL

makes one 11-by-4-inch bûche de Noël

Growing up, our family's Christmas Eve dinner was always followed with a Yule log, and it seemed only fitting to create this Francophile version for Miette. I love that the bûche de Noël is a celebration of winter and our cake looks like a quiet woodland scene, complete with pinecones, holly leaves, and meringue mushrooms.

This cake is difficult to assemble so you must space out the process. You start at the end: Make your decorations first and store them in an airtight container for up to 1 month. Then, bake the cake, make the mousse, and roll it all on the same day. Wrap tightly with plastic wrap and keep in the freezer (protected from anything that might damage the shape) overnight or for up to 2 weeks.

ingredients

1 CHOCOLATE CHIFFON CAKE (PAGE 72), STILL ATTACHED TO PARCHMENT

ABOUT 3 CUPS CHOCOLATE MOUSSE (PAGE 197)

ABOUT 2 CUPS CHOCOLATE GANACHE (PAGE 195)

MERINGUE MUSHROOMS (PAGE 174) FOR GARNISH

OPTIONAL DECORATIONS: MARZIPAN HOLLY LEAVES AND BERRIES, SANDING SUGAR, CHOCOLATE PINECONES (SEE SOURCES, PAGE 218)

preparation

1. Read through or review the "Cake Assembly and Decorating Basics" section beginning on page 21.

2. Make the Chocolate Chiffon Cake as directed and make sure it is cool inside and out. (If frozen, let thaw in the refrigerator, 3 to 4 hours. If time demands, you can thaw on the countertop, 1 to 2 hours, but be careful not to let it sit too much longer before you begin working with it, as the texture will lose quality.)

3. Clear a space in the freezer large enough for a baking sheet to hold the rolled 11-by-4-inch bûche, giving it plenty of space to lie flat and keep its nice round shape. Make the mousse as directed.

4. Position the rectangle of chiffon cake so that the long edge is perpendicular to the edge of the counter. Using an offset spatula, spread the mousse in an even layer across the cake, leaving a 1-inch border uncovered around the edges.

5. With the parchment paper still attached, starting with the short edge closest to you, start to roll the cake away from you, tucking it into the mousse and creating a tight first turn. The first tuck is important because it determines the shape of the finished roll. Once you are happy with the positioning of the first turn, peel back the exposed parchment and use it to lift the cake into the next turn. You should be about two-thirds of the way to the end of the cake. Now, grab the far end of the cake and pull it toward you, keeping the parchment intact. Tuck it snugly against the bottom of the cake. Push the roll away from you a bit as you hold on to the exposed piece of parchment, creating tension. This makes your roll nice and tight. Take up the exposed/ excess parchment and wrap it tightly around the chiffon bûche. Roll the log in plastic wrap, twisting the ends to hold its shape. Place on a baking sheet and carefully transport to the freezer and let set up over- night, or for up to 2 weeks.

6. The day you plan to serve it, remove the bûche from the freezer. The cake is easiest to decorate when frozen and will have defrosted by the time you are ready to serve it. Place on a wire rack set over a rimmed baking sheet or jelly-roll pan. Clear a space in the refrigerator large enough for the bûche on the baking sheet.

7. Scoop the ganache into a microwave-safe bowl. (If the ganache was made earlier and has been chilled to a solid, first microwave on high for 1 minute. Stir very gently so as not to agitate the chocolate, which would introduce air.) Microwave at 10-second intervals, gently stirring between each, until the ganache is mostly liquid. Have ready an immer- sion blender, which you will use to make the glaze very smooth and pourable. Add about 2 tablespoons very hot water to the ganache, and let the water sit on top. Insert the head of the blender, while it is off, into the ganache very slowly at a 45-degree angle; you do not want to trap any air in the compartment of the head. When the head of the blender is submerged, twist the blender to a 90-degree angle and turn it on.

continued

Begin to make gentle circles, never up and down and never breaking the surface, until the chocolate is very shiny and smooth, 3 to 5 minutes. Be patient, as you will need more time than you think. When you begin to see a shine develop, you think you are done, but go on a little longer.

8.   Slowly pour the glaze over the log, beginning at one end and working toward the other. This helps to ensure an even coat all over the cake. Rap the tray lightly on the table to settle the glaze. Refrigerate until set, about 30 minutes.

9.   Repeat the glazing step once more, scraping up the extra ganache from the baking sheet and making sure to repeat the process above to restore the glaze to its shiniest level. Return to the refrigerator for about 15 minutes.

10. Place a long serrated knife in a tall container of hot water. Remove the bûche from the refrigerator and run the backside of the tines of a fork along the cake lengthwise in a slightly wavy pattern. Repeat all over the cake so that it looks like bark. Dry the heated knife and use to trim ½ inch off both ends of the cake, wiping the blade clean between cuts.

11. Carefully transfer the cake to a presentation platter or plate by first running a knife around the perimeter of the cake and then inserting a large spatula under the cake edge to lift, making sure not to rip the chocolate from the rack. Transfer to the refrigerator and let set for 30 minutes or up to overnight. (Scrape any remaining ganache off the baking sheet and save it for another use.)

12. Remove from the refrigerator 30 minutes before serving. Decorate with the mushrooms. Add any additional decorations, as desired. (The sanding sugar creates a charming snow effect.)

YELLOW CUPCAKES

makes 18 cupcakes

All the other cupcakes at Miette are made from the same batters that go into the larger cakes. This recipe, however, was developed just to be a cupcake.

And of all the recipes at Miette, the innocent-seeming yellow classic cupcake took the most time to figure out. I had just hired a new head baker, and I am very surprised she didn't quit in her first week because of this recipe. The challenge was to produce a moist yellow cupcake with lots of flavor but also enough body to hold up to a rich buttercream frosting. I wanted the flavor of butter to shine but when we tried to make cupcakes from our Butter Cake batter (see page 48) the cupcakes came out with a dense crumb, and when paired with buttercream, the combination was simply too rich. We finally solved the mystery: replace a portion of the all-purpose flour with potato starch. The starch sustains the structure of the cupcake while providing a fine crumb, creating a light, fluffy cake that still tastes buttery.

At the bakery, we pair this cupcake with strawberry, chocolate, lemon, and vanilla buttercreams and decorate with candied flowers.

ingredients

1 CUP (8 OUNCES) UNSALTED BUTTER

½ CUP MILK

3 LARGE EGGS

2 TEASPOONS VANILLA EXTRACT

1½ CUPS (7½ OUNCES) ALL-PURPOSE FLOUR

1⅓ CUPS (8½ OUNCES) SUGAR

¼ CUP (1½ OUNCES) POTATO STARCH

2 TEASPOONS BAKING POWDER

1 TEASPOON KOSHER SALT

ABOUT 3 CUPS VANILLA, LEMON, RASPBERRY, CHOCOLATE, OR OTHER BUTTERCREAM (PAGES 185–189)

18 SUGAR LEAVES AND CANDIED FLOWERS FOR GARNISH (OPTIONAL; SEE SOURCES, PAGE 218)

preparation

1. Read through or review the "Cake-Baking Essentials" section beginning on page 18.

2. Line 18 standard cupcake cups with paper liners. Preheat the oven to 350 degrees F.

3. In a saucepan over medium-low heat, combine the butter and milk and heat, stirring occasionally, until the butter is melted, 3 to 4 minutes. Alternatively, in a microwave-safe bowl, combine the butter and milk and microwave on high at 10-second intervals, stirring between each, until the butter is melted. Set aside and let cool to slightly above room temperature; an instant-read thermometer should register between 80 and 85 degrees F.

continued

4. In a microwave-safe bowl, whisk the eggs with the vanilla. Microwave on low for 30-second intervals, stirring between each, until the egg mixture reaches 80 to 85 degrees F on the thermometer. Alternatively, heat the mixture, whisking, in the top pan of a double boiler or in a bowl for a bain-marie placed over (but not touching) simmering water.

5. Combine the flour, sugar, potato starch, baking powder, and salt in the bowl of a stand mixer fitted with the paddle attachment. Begin mixing on low speed, then slowly drizzle in the milk mixture. Beat until just combined. With the mixer set on low speed, add the egg mixture in three additions, beating until just incorporated between additions. The batter should be silky and smooth and very liquid.

6. Fill each cupcake liner two-thirds full with batter (it works well to use a ¼-cup measure; don't scrape it out each time, just drop the batter in). Bake until nicely risen and golden brown, 20 to 23 minutes. Immediately transfer the cupcakes from the pans to wire racks and let cool completely, about 30 minutes.

7. To decorate the cupcakes, fit a pastry bag with a medium (½- or ⅝-inch) star tip and fill the bag about halfway with the buttercream. Pull up the cuff and twist it to seal and tighten the frosting down into the cone. Purge the bag of air bubbles by squeezing the bag until there is a burst of air and frosting sputters out of the bag. Keep the bag tightly twisted so that the frosting doesn't come back up on your hands. Starting at the edge of a cupcake at a 90-degree angle and about ½ inch from the top, pipe a spiral toward the middle, ending with a point in the center. Add a sugar leaf and candied flower to the point, if desired. Repeat to frost the remaining cupcakes.

CHEESECAKE

makes one 6-inch cake

For years, our customers asked me to make a cheesecake, but it took me a long time to figure out how to make a Miette version. Since cheesecake is greatly about the crust, the inspiration finally came when we created the graham cracker crust for our Lime Meringue Tart (page 111). To make the definitive Miette cheesecake, you must make our Graham Crackers, then crumble them into fine golden crumbs. You can make an equally delicious chocolate crust using our Chocolate Wafer Cookies.

The texture of the cheesecake filling is perfectly smooth and light without being airy—a quality we achieve with our mantra of "strain, strain, strain." Simply pouring the batter through a sieve removes even small lumps of cream cheese and delivers a satiny texture. The other key to our cake is that we use high-quality organic cream cheese, which is denser than regular cream cheese and has a mellower flavor. As in many cheesecake recipes, the cake is baked in a bain-marie. If you have ever been daunted by this step or skipped it, do not; the time-tested

continued

ingredients

¾ CUP GRAHAM CRACKER CRUMBS (PAGE 152) OR CHOCOLATE WAFER CRUMBS (PAGE 127)

1 POUND CREAM CHEESE, AT ROOM TEMPERATURE

½ CUP (3½ OUNCES) SUGAR

2 LARGE EGGS

¼ CUP HEAVY CREAM

¾ TEASPOON VANILLA EXTRACT

GLAZE

½ CUP (4 OUNCES) SOUR CREAM

1 TABLESPOON SUGAR

preparation

1. Read through or review the "Cake-Baking Essentials" section beginning on page 18.

2. Preheat the oven to 350 degrees F.

3. Put the graham cracker crumbs in a 6-inch springform pan and press in an even layer on the bottom. Bake the crust until dark golden brown and firm, 8 to 10 minutes. Transfer to a wire rack and let cool. Leave the oven on.

4. When the crust is cool, wrap the bottom of the pan with plastic wrap and place in the oven for 3 minutes to shrink the plastic. (This will prevent the water in the bain-marie from entering the pan during baking.) Return to the wire rack to cool. Still leave the oven on.

continued

technique promotes even cooking and prevents the cheesecake from browning on the sides. The goal is a pristine, white, creamy cake.

5. In the bowl of a stand mixer fitted with the paddle attachment, beat the cream cheese on medium speed until fluffy but without adding too much air, until smooth and creamy, without any lumps, 5 to 8 minutes. Gradually add the sugar and beat until smooth. Stop the mixer.

6. With the mixer set on low speed, drop the eggs, one at a time, into the cream cheese mixture. Beat each egg until thoroughly incorporated before adding the next. Slowly add the cream and then the vanilla and beat until smooth, 5 to 8 minutes.

7. Strain the batter through a medium-mesh sieve into a clean bowl, then pour into the cooled crust.

8. Bring a large kettle of water to a boil.

9. Place the filled cheesecake pan in a roasting pan. Carefully pour the boiling water into the larger pan to reach halfway up the sides of the cheesecake pan. Bake until the filling is set and just barely jiggles in the center, about 1 hour and 30 minutes. Remove from the water bath and place on the wire rack to cool completely.

10. To make the glaze: Add the sour cream and sugar to a small bowl and whisk to combine. Spread it over the top of the cooled cheesecake.

11. Wrap tightly with plastic wrap and refrigerate for at least 2 hours and up to 8 hours. Remove from the refrigerator 30 minutes before serving.

    To de-pan and serve, unlatch the springform pan and use an offset spatula to loosen the crust from the pan and transfer to a cake board.

afternoon cakes

Pumpkin-Walnut Cake
85

Carrot Cake
88

Lemon Tea Cake
92

Honey Tea Cake
94

Banana Bread with Nutty Streusel
96

Gingerbread
98

AFTERNOON CAKES

The six cakes in this chapter go back to the days when we were just a tent at the Berkeley Farmers' Market, and thus limited to cakes that could travel well and did not require refrigeration. We were at the farmers' market for two years before we moved into our shop at the Ferry Building, and in those years we experimented with many recipes; these are the ones that held up to the test of time. They belong to a category we call "Picnickers," because they are sturdy enough to toss in the picnic basket and moist enough to last the weekend without special care. They are rich in character and flavor, dense and moist, and can host the variety of seasonal nuts and flavors without elaborate decoration other than a simple frosting or glaze.

These cakes aren't as fancy as the cakes in the previous chapter, but they are equally delicious, easy to make, and perfect for more casual occasions, served at lunch or in the afternoon with a cup of tea.

PUMPKIN-WALNUT CAKE

makes one 10-inch bundt cake

Every spring, Annabelle Lenderink of La Tercera Farm in Marin County sows seeds for a particular kind of pumpkin specifically for this cake of ours. Throughout the summer, it delights me to think about my pumpkins, called Galeux d'Eysines, growing in their special plot of land in Bolinas, at the very tip of the San Andreas Fault. This variety of pumpkin is not known for the beauty of its outer skin, which is covered in warts and bumps. Indeed, the first year Annabelle grew the Galeux, at the end of the market she had plenty left over that did not sell. I took them back to the bakery and discovered just how gorgeous this pumpkin is for baking. The flavor is subtle and earthy, with a high water content that gives the cake a light and delicate crumb, distinguishing it from the average pumpkin loaf, which is often dense as a brick. You can make a purée from any variety of small sugar pumpkins or use canned pumpkin; stir in ¼ cup water to loosen the purée. This cake can also be made in two 8-by-4-inch loaf pans, following the instructions for Carrot Cake (page 88). It is delicious glazed with Chocolate Ganache.

ingredients

1¾ CUPS (9 OUNCES) ALL-PURPOSE FLOUR

1½ TEASPOONS BAKING SODA

2 TEASPOONS GROUND CINNAMON

1 TEASPOON GROUND NUTMEG

½ TEASPOON GROUND CLOVES

¾ TEASPOON KOSHER SALT

4 LARGE EGGS

1⅔ CUPS (12 OUNCES) SUGAR

1 CUP VEGETABLE OIL

1¾ CUPS HOMEMADE PUMPKIN PURÉE (SEE NOTE) OR ONE 14-OUNCE CAN PURE SOLID-PACK PUMPKIN MIXED WITH ¼ CUP WATER

1 CUP (3½ OUNCES) SMALL WALNUT PIECES, TOASTED

¼ CUP CHOCOLATE GANACHE (PAGE 195; OPTIONAL)

preparation

1. Read through or review the "Cake-Baking Essentials" section beginning on page 18.

2. Liberally butter a 10-inch bundt pan and dust with flour. Tap out the excess flour.

3. Preheat the oven to 350 degrees F.

4. Sift together the flour, baking soda, cinnamon, nutmeg, cloves, and salt into a bowl and set aside.

continued

5. In the bowl of a stand mixer fitted with the whisk attachment, combine the eggs and sugar and whisk on medium speed until well combined and lightened in color, about 2 minutes. Reduce the speed to low, slowly drizzle in the oil, and whisk until combined, then whisk on high speed for 1 minute to emulsify.

6. Switch to the paddle attachment. Add the pumpkin purée to the egg mixture and mix on medium speed just until combined. Add the dry ingredients in three additions, mixing just until combined after each addition, approximately 5 seconds each time. Remove the bowl from the mixer and scrape down the sides with a rubber spatula. Fold in the walnuts by hand.

7. Pour the batter into the prepared pan. Bake until the cake springs back when touched and a tester inserted in the center comes out clean, 45 to 50 minutes. Transfer to a wire rack and cool in the pan for 10 minutes. Run an offset spatula around the edges of the pan, then invert the cake onto the rack and let cool for about 20 minutes longer. Serve right away, or wrap tightly in plastic wrap and refrigerate until you are ready to serve and up to 3 days. To freeze, wrap tightly in a second layer of plastic and store in the freezer for up to 2 months. Serve at room temperature.

note

To make your own pumpkin purée, preheat the oven to 400 degrees F. Scrub a small (about 4 pounds) sugar pumpkin well and wipe dry. Cut the pumpkin in half and place the halves, flesh-side down, on a greased cookie sheet and bake until very soft, about 1 hour. Let the pumpkin cool. Scrape out the seeds and stringy fibers and discard. Scoop out the flesh of the pumpkin and process until smooth in a food processor or pass through a food mill to make a purée. Makes about 2½ cups purée.

CARROT CAKE

makes three small 5-inch loaves or one 7-inch round cake

You can taste the cinnamon in Miette's carrot cake, a very moist version studded with chewy sweet currants, walnuts, and shredded coconut. We originally sold this cake only in small loaves; however, our customers complained that it disappeared too quickly and demanded a cake. Now, in addition to the loaf-pan sizes allowed for here, we also bake our beloved carrot-cake batter into a cupcake (see the variation on page 91) and one single-layer, 7-inch round cake, all with a classic sweet and dense Cream Cheese Frosting.

ingredients

1 CUP (5 OUNCES) ALL-PURPOSE FLOUR

1 TEASPOON BAKING SODA

1 TEASPOON BAKING POWDER

1 TEASPOON GROUND CINNAMON

½ TEASPOON KOSHER SALT

2 LARGE EGGS, AT ROOM TEMPERATURE

1 CUP (7 OUNCES) SUGAR

¾ CUP VEGETABLE OIL

1 CUP (8 OUNCES) PEELED AND FINELY SHREDDED CARROTS

½ CUP (2½ OUNCES) CURRANTS

½ CUP (2 OUNCES) WALNUT PIECES, TOASTED

½ CUP (1½ OUNCES) SHREDDED DRIED COCONUT

ABOUT 2 CUPS CREAM CHEESE FROSTING (PAGE 191)

preparation

1. Read through or review the "Cake-Baking Essentials" section beginning on page 18.

2. Liberally butter three 5-by-3-inch loaf pans or one 7-by-2-inch cake pan and dust with sifted flour. Tap out the excess flour.

3. Preheat the oven to 350 degrees F.

4. Sift together the flour, baking soda, baking powder, cinnamon, and salt into a bowl and set aside.

5. In the bowl of a stand mixer fitted with the whisk attachment, combine the eggs and sugar. Whisk on medium speed until well combined and lightened in color, about 2 minutes. Reduce the speed to low, slowly drizzle in the oil, and whisk until combined, then whisk on high speed for 1 minute to emulsify.

6. Switch to the paddle attachment. Add the dry ingredients in three additions and beat on medium speed until smooth, about 2 minutes. Add the carrots, currants, walnuts, and coconut and beat just to combine. Remove the bowl from the mixer and scrape down the sides with a rubber spatula. Fold by hand a few more times with the spatula, scraping the bottom of the bowl to bring the currants up from the bottom.

7. Divide the batter between the prepared pans. Bake until the tops of the loaves are golden brown and a tester inserted in the center comes out clean, 20 to 25 minutes for the small loaves and 40 to 45 minutes for the 7-inch cake. Transfer to wire racks and let cool in the pans for 20 minutes. Run an offset spatula around the edges of the pans, then invert the cakes onto the racks and let cool for about 20 minutes longer. Wrap tightly in plastic wrap and refrigerate to ensure that the interiors are completely cooled before decorating, at least 1 hour or up to 3 days. To freeze, wrap tightly in a second layer of plastic and store in the freezer for up to 2 months.

8. To decorate the carrot cakes, fit a pastry bag with a medium (½- or ⅝-inch) star tip and fill the bag with the frosting. Pull up the cuff and twist it to seal and tighten the frosting down into the cone. Purge the bag of air bubbles by squeezing the bag until there is a burst of air and frosting sputters out of the bag. Keep the bag tightly twisted so that the frosting doesn't come back up on your hands. Starting in the center of each cake, holding the pastry bag at a 90-degree angle, pipe frosting in a tight (loaf-shaped in the case of the small cakes) spiral over the top of each. Use an offset spatula to partially smooth the surface of the frosting, leaving some pretty contours at the edges for visual interest. Serve at room temperature.

continued

CARROT CUPCAKES

1. Line two dozen standard muffin cups with paper liners. Fill each cupcake liner two-thirds full with batter (it works well to use a ¼-cup measure; don't scrape it out each time, just drop the batter in). Bake in a 350-degree-F oven until the tops spring back and a tester inserted in the center of a cupcake comes out clean, 20 to 25 minutes. Immediately transfer the cupcakes from the pans to wire racks to cool.

2. To decorate, fit a pastry bag with a medium (½- or ⅝-inch) star tip and fill the bag halfway with the frosting. Pull up the cuff and twist it to seal and tighten the frosting down into the cone. Purge the bag of air bubbles by squeezing the bag until there is a burst of air and frosting sputters out of the bag. Keep the bag tightly twisted so that the frosting doesn't come back up on your hands. Starting about ½ inch from the edge of a cupcake and holding the bag at a 90-degree angle, pipe a spiral toward the middle, ending with a point in the center. Add a sugar flower and leaf to the point, if desired (see Sources, page 218). Makes 18 to 24 cupcakes.

LEMON TEA CAKE

makes four small 5-inch loaves or two standard 8-inch loaves

At the Ferry Building, this lemon cake (pictured on page 82) sits on a shelf that faces the nave—easy to grab if you're en route to home or the office. One by one, our customers buy them up and by the end of the hectic lunch rush, they are all gone.

I romanticize the pound cake, feeling it deserves to be made with ample respect for the traditional recipe. However, a true pound cake (so called at its conception because it was made with 1 pound of each ingredient) is far too dense; the Miette version is by comparison quite modern, and benefits from being significantly lighter. Still, there is plenty of butter, egg yolks, and cream to make it every bit as moist and satisfying as you expect in a perfect pound cake. For an extra-deep lemon flavor, we brush it with lemon syrup while it's still hot from the oven, and then ice it with a tart lemon glaze. We package this cake in a cellophane bag and tie it with a green bow, making it ideal to toss in the picnic basket.

ingredients

2½ CUPS (12 OUNCES) ALL-PURPOSE FLOUR

1½ CUPS (10½ OUNCES) GRANULATED SUGAR

2½ TEASPOONS BAKING POWDER

½ TEASPOON KOSHER SALT

1 CUP HEAVY CREAM

7 LARGE EGG YOLKS

2 LARGE WHOLE EGGS

1½ TEASPOONS VANILLA EXTRACT

2½ TABLESPOONS GRATED LEMON ZEST

1⅓ CUPS (11 OUNCES) UNSALTED BUTTER, CUBED

½ CUP LEMON SIMPLE SYRUP (PAGE 207)

LEMON GLAZE

2 TABLESPOONS FRESHLY SQUEEZED LEMON JUICE

1 TEASPOON CORN SYRUP

1⅓ CUPS (7 OUNCES) SIFTED POWDERED SUGAR

preparation

1. Read through or review the "Cake-Baking Essentials" section beginning on page 18.

2. Liberally butter four 5-by-3-inch or two 8-by-4-inch loaf pans and dust with sifted flour. Tap out the excess flour.

3. Preheat the oven to 350 degrees F.

4. In a medium bowl, sift together the flour, granulated sugar, baking powder, and salt. Set aside.

5. In a small bowl, stir together the cream, egg yolks, whole eggs, vanilla, and lemon zest. Set aside.

6. In the bowl of a stand mixer fitted with the paddle attachment, mix the dry ingredients on medium speed for 30 seconds. Reduce the speed to low, add the butter, and mix for 1 minute. Add half of the egg mixture and beat until incorporated, about 1 minute. Add the remaining egg mixture, and beat just until incorporated, 1 to 2 minutes longer.

7. Divide the batter between the prepared pans. Bake until the tops of the loaves are golden brown and a tester inserted in the center comes out clean, about 45 minutes for the small loaves and 55 minutes for the larger loaves. Transfer to wire racks and immediately brush the tops with the lemon syrup. Let cool in the pans for about 20 minutes. Run an offset spatula around the edges of the pans, then invert the cakes onto the racks and let cool for about 20 minutes longer. (To freeze, wrap the cakes tightly in plastic wrap and store in the freezer for up to 2 months. Thaw at room temperature.)

8. Meanwhile, make the glaze: In a small bowl, whisk together the lemon juice and corn syrup. Sprinkle in the powdered sugar, a little at a time, whisking constantly, until the glaze is thick and silky. You may not need all of the sugar. Glaze the cooled cakes and let the glaze dry, about 30 minutes.

9. Serve right away, or wrap the cakes tightly in plastic wrap and store at room temperature until ready to serve.

HONEY TEA CAKE

makes four small 5-inch loaves or two standard 8-inch loaves

This cake was inspired by my infatuation with honey—along with the notion that something so delicious would shine even more in the company of butter. The kind of honey you use will influence the flavor, so experiment with the many artisan honeys that are becoming more and more available at farmers' markets and specialty markets, flavored by the local flowers from which the bees sip. We use an organic local honey that has a mild floral taste.

ingredients

2⅔ CUPS (12 OUNCES) ALL-PURPOSE FLOUR

2 TEASPOONS BAKING POWDER

1 TEASPOON KOSHER SALT

8 LARGE EGG YOLKS

2 LARGE WHOLE EGGS

1 CUP HEAVY CREAM

1 TEASPOON VANILLA EXTRACT

1½ CUPS (11 OUNCES) SUGAR

1 CUP PLUS 6 TABLESPOONS (11 OUNCES) UNSALTED BUTTER, AT ROOM TEMPERATURE

¼ CUP HONEY, WARMED AND DILUTED WITH 2 TABLESPOONS WATER TO MAKE A SYRUP

preparation

1. Read through or review the "Cake-Baking Essentials" section beginning on page 18.

2. Liberally butter four 5-by-3-inch or two 8-by-4-inch loaf pans and dust with flour. Tap out the excess flour.

3. Preheat the oven to 350 degrees F.

4. Sift together the flour, baking powder, and salt into a small bowl. In another small bowl, stir together the egg yolks, whole eggs, cream, and vanilla.

5. In the bowl of a stand mixer fitted with the paddle attachment, combine the dry ingredients and the sugar and mix on medium speed for 30 seconds. Reduce the speed to low, add the butter and half of the egg mixture, and beat until incorporated, about 2 minutes. Raise the speed to medium-high and beat for 2 minutes to add air to build structure. Return the speed to low, add the remaining egg mixture, and beat just until incorporated, 2 to 3 minutes longer.

6. Divide the batter between the prepared pans. Bake until the tops of the loaves are golden brown and a tester inserted in the center comes out clean, 20 to 25 minutes for the small loaves and 35 to 40 minutes for the larger loaves.

7. Transfer to wire racks and immediately brush the tops or drizzle with the honey syrup. Let cool in the pans for 20 minutes. Run an offset spatula around the edges of the pans, invert the cakes onto the racks, and let cool for about 20 minutes longer. Serve right away, or wrap the cakes tightly in plastic wrap and store at room temperature until ready to serve, or refrigerate for 3 days. To freeze, wrap tightly in a second layer of plastic and store in the freezer for up to 2 months. To thaw, leave in the refrigerator for 3 to 4 hours or on the countertop for 1 to 2 hours. Serve at room temperature.

BANANA BREAD WITH NUTTY STREUSEL

makes four small 5-inch loaves or two standard 8-inch loaves

Full of pecans, butter, and brown sugar, the nutty streusel in this recipe was the obsession that led to Miette's beloved version of banana tea cake—a bit like getting dressed from the socks up. I asked my staff to come up with different ideas for using streusel and we had a bake-off. The banana bread was a clear winner, with the added benefit of helping us use up a continual stash of overripe bananas.

Delicate in texture, it is more of a cake than a bread and full of banana flavor. Once, one of our sly bakers put chocolate chips in the batter when I wasn't looking, and I have to admit, they are a great addition. But there are times when you want something without chocolate, so here is the pure version.

NUTTY STREUSEL

½ CUP (2 OUNCES) PECAN PIECES

¼ CUP (2 OUNCES) SUGAR

⅓ CUP (1½ OUNCES) ALL-PURPOSE FLOUR

2 TABLESPOONS COLD UNSALTED BUTTER

¾ TEASPOON GROUND CINNAMON

¼ TEASPOON VANILLA EXTRACT

⅛ TEASPOON KOSHER SALT

BANANA BREAD

2¼ CUPS (11 OUNCES) ALL-PURPOSE FLOUR

1 TEASPOON BAKING SODA

¾ TEASPOON BAKING POWDER

1 TEASPOON KOSHER SALT

1½ CUPS (11 OUNCES) SUGAR

2 LARGE EGGS

1 TEASPOON VANILLA EXTRACT

½ CUP VEGETABLE OIL

4 MEDIUM SOFT, BUT NOT BLACK, BANANAS (ABOUT 1 POUND TOTAL), PEELED AND ROUGHLY MASHED

½ CUP (2 OUNCES) PECAN PIECES

1. Read through or review the "Cake-Baking Essentials" section beginning on page 18.

2. Liberally butter four 5-by-3-inch or two 8-by-4-inch loaf pans and dust with sifted flour. Tap out the excess flour.

3. Preheat the oven to 350 degrees F.

4. To make the streusel: In a food processor, add the pecans, sugar, flour, butter, cinnamon, vanilla, and salt and pulse until coarsely combined. Transfer to a small bowl, cover, and refrigerate until ready to use, up to 5 days.

5. To make the banana bread: Sift together the flour, baking soda, baking powder, and salt into a bowl and set aside.

6. In the bowl of a stand mixer fitted with the whisk attachment, whisk the sugar, eggs, and vanilla on medium speed until well combined and lightened in color, 4 to 5 minutes. Reduce the speed to low and drizzle in the oil, whisking just until combined. Add the banana mash and whisk just until combined. Add the dry ingredients and pecans to the batter in three additions, whisking just to combine after each addition. Do not overmix.

7. Divide the batter between the prepared pans. Sprinkle the tops with the streusel, dividing it evenly. (You may not need all of the streusel if making the smaller loaves.) Bake until the breads have risen nicely and a tester inserted in the center comes out clean, 40 to 45 minutes for the small loaves and 45 to 50 minutes for the larger loaves. Transfer to wire racks and let cool in the pans for 20 minutes. Run an offset spatula around the edges of the pans, then invert the cakes onto the racks and let cool for about 20 minutes longer. Serve right away, or wrap tightly in plastic wrap and refrigerate until you are ready to serve, up to 3 days. To freeze, wrap tightly in a second layer of plastic and store in the freezer for up to 2 months. Serve at room temperature.

GINGERBREAD

makes four small 5-inch loaves or two 7-inch cakes

Miette's gingerbread cake started as a seasonal cake, arriving with the crisp days of fall. But when we tried to cycle it out, there was so much demand that we made it available year-round. It remains our best-selling cake, very moist, deeply spicy, and topped with a silky cream cheese frosting. We bake it as a small cake, but you can also prepare it in small loaf pans.

To make this gingerbread, you boil the molasses and beer together and then add baking soda. The baking soda causes the mixture to expand rapidly, so add it very slowly to prevent the brew from going over the sides of your pot. Truth be told, the brew smells awful, but it's the potion that makes the cake moist and flavorful. You can prepare the brew up to 5 days in advance; store it tightly covered in the refrigerator.

This cake is sensitive to being overmixed, which has the effect of making it develop too much height and as a result, it won't bake well. To avoid overmixing, we just strain out any lumps in the batter before the final pour into the pans.

ingredients

1¼ CUPS (6½ OUNCES) ALL-PURPOSE FLOUR

1 TEASPOON BAKING POWDER

1 TABLESPOON PLUS 2 TEASPOONS GROUND GINGER

¾ TEASPOON GROUND CINNAMON

¼ TEASPOON GROUND CLOVES

¼ TEASPOON GROUND NUTMEG

⅛ TEASPOON GROUND CARDAMOM

¼ TEASPOON KOSHER SALT

½ CUP PLUS 2 TABLESPOONS STOUT BEER, SUCH AS GUINNESS

¾ CUP MOLASSES

½ TEASPOON BAKING SODA

2 LARGE EGGS, AT ROOM TEMPERATURE

¾ CUP (5½ OUNCES) GRANULATED SUGAR

½ CUP (4 OUNCES) LIGHT BROWN SUGAR, PACKED

½ CUP VEGETABLE OIL

ABOUT 2 CUPS CREAM CHEESE FROSTING (PAGE 191)

PINK SUGAR FLOWERS FOR GARNISH (OPTIONAL; SEE SOURCES, PAGE 218)

preparation

1. Read through or review the "Cake-Baking Essentials" section beginning on page 18.

2. Liberally butter four 5-by-3-inch loaf pans or two 7-by-2-inch cake pans and dust with flour. Tap out the excess flour.

continued

3. Preheat the oven to 350 degrees F.

4. Sift together the flour, baking powder, spices, and salt into a bowl and set aside.

5. In a small saucepan over medium heat, stir together the stout and molasses and bring to a boil. Whisk in the baking soda. Be careful and whisk constantly, as the mixture will foam up when you add the soda. Immediately remove from the heat and let the mixture cool to room temperature.

6. In the bowl of a stand mixer fitted with the whisk attachment, combine the eggs and granulated and brown sugars and whisk on medium speed until well combined and lightened in color, 3 to 4 minutes. Slowly drizzle in the oil and beat until combined. Reduce the speed to low and slowly add the stout mixture. Stop the mixer and scrape down the sides of the bowl with a rubber spatula, then return to low speed and slowly add the dry ingredients, beating just until combined. Remove the bowl from the mixer and scrape down the sides with a rubber spatula. Fold by hand a few more times with the spatula. Strain the batter through a medium-mesh sieve into a clean bowl. Divide it between the prepared pans.

7. Bake until nicely risen and lightly browned at the edges, about 35 minutes for the loaves and 45 to 50 minutes for the cakes. (Check the loaves at 25 minutes.) Transfer to wire racks and let cool in the pans for 20 minutes. Run an offset spatula around the edges of the pans, then invert the cakes onto the racks and let cool for about 20 minutes longer. Wrap tightly in plastic wrap and refrigerate to ensure that the interiors are completely cooled before decorating, at least 1 hour or up to 3 days. To freeze, wrap tightly in a second layer of plastic and store in the freezer for up to 2 months.

8. To decorate the gingerbread, fit a pastry bag with a medium (½- or ⅝-inch) star tip and fill the bag with the frosting. Pull up the cuff and twist it to seal and tighten the frosting down into the cone. Purge the bag of air bubbles by squeezing the bag until there is a burst of air and frosting sputters out of the bag. Keep the bag tightly twisted so that the frosting doesn't come back up on your hands. Starting in the center of each loaf or cake, pipe frosting in a tight spiral over the surface. Use an offset spatula to slightly smooth the surface of the frosting. Garnish with a pink sugar flower or two, if you like. Serve at room temperature.

GINGERBREAD CUPCAKES

1. Line two dozen standard muffin cups with paper liners. Fill each cupcake liner two-thirds full with batter (it works well to use a ¼-cup measure; don't scrape it out each time, just drop the batter in). Bake at 350 degrees F until the tops spring back and a tester inserted in the center of a cupcake comes out clean, 20 to 25 minutes. Immediately transfer the cupcakes from the pans to wire racks to cool.

2. To decorate, fit a pastry bag with a medium (½- or ⅝-inch) star tip and fill the bag with frosting. Pull up the cuff and twist it to seal and tighten the frosting down into the cone. Purge the bag of air bubbles by squeezing the bag until there is a burst of air and frosting sputters out of the bag. Keep the bag tightly twisted so that the frosting doesn't come back up on your hands. Starting about ½ inch from the edge of a cupcake and holding the pastry bag at a 90-degree angle, pipe a rosette, ending with a point in the center. Place a sugar flower on the point, if you like. Makes 18 to 24 cupcakes.

tarts

Pâte Sucrée Tart Shell
105

Chocolate Truffle Tart
107

Lime Meringue Tart
111

Lemon Tart
114

Pastry Cream and Fresh Fruit Tart
115

Banana Cream Tart
118

Pecan Tart
120

TARTS

At Miette, the tarts herald in the seasons from their position on the top shelf of our pastry case. The Lemon Tart (page 114) carries us through a California winter, Pastry Cream and Fresh Fruit Tarts (page 115) welcome the spring, and blueberry or raspberry tartlettes celebrate the height of summer. When the last summer fruits are finished, we switch to pecans and other autumnal flavors. The tarts and tartlettes in this section are simple and elegant, featuring the intense flavors of the fillings bound in a crisp buttery shell.

With the exception of the Lime Meringue Tart (page 111), all of our tart shells use Pâte Sucrée (see page 105), a dough that is really a shortbread with a rich uniform crumb permeated with butter; and, like a shortbread, the dough is more tender the less it is worked. For an especially rich flavor, be sure to bake the tart shells to a dark golden brown color. It brings out their buttery flavor and looks far more beautiful than a pallid, under-baked crust. Note: It is crucial that the filling is cold and the crust is cooled before you fill the tarts. A warm crust will melt the filling, making the crust soggy.

We bake our tarts in a 7-inch tart pan. Each recipe includes a tartlette variation.

The tart shells can be made up to 2 days ahead, which makes a fresh, beautiful tart the ideal party fare—especially the tartlettes, which are elegant individual desserts. You can serve the tarts either at room temperature or cold, depending on your preference. Always store tarts in the refrigerator.

PÂTE SUCRÉE TART SHELL

makes enough for two 7-inch tarts or ten 3½-inch tartlettes (about 1 pound)

A tart is no greater than its crust, and a good crust is tender, crumbly, and baked until golden brown. Pâte sucrée is similar to a rich, buttery pie dough, but the texture is rather more like shortbread than flaky. We use our version of this time-honored crust for all but one of our tarts. Its buttery flavor is incredibly versatile and a wonderful complement to all our fillings.

Another advantage to pâte sucrée is that it holds up to moisture, so tarts don't get soggy even after they've been filled for a day. The unusual ingredient is egg yolk, which gives the dough richness while keeping it tender. It goes without saying (but I'll say it again anyway) that the quality of the butter you use is essential—use the best, richest butter you can find.

Once you make the dough and line your pan, you need to pre-bake it before you fill it. For fillings that also need to cook, you first partially pre-bake the crust to make it sturdier—a brief stint in the oven activates the chemistry needed to crisp the crust and create a barrier for holding juices—and then finish

continued

ingredients

3⅓ CUPS (16 OUNCES) ALL-PURPOSE FLOUR

¼ CUP (2 OUNCES) SUGAR

½ TEASPOON SALT

1 CUP (8 OUNCES) COLD UNSALTED BUTTER, CUBED

2 LARGE EGG YOLKS

4 TO 8 TABLESPOONS HEAVY CREAM

preparation

1. In the bowl of a stand mixer fitted with the paddle attachment, combine the flour, sugar, and salt. Mix on low speed for 30 seconds. Add the butter and beat until the mixture is the consistency of cornmeal, about 5 minutes.

2. In a small bowl, whisk together the egg yolks and 2 tablespoons of the cream. Add to the flour mixture and mix until just combined. If the dough does not come together into large chunks, slowly add the remaining cream, a little bit at a time, until it does. Gather the dough into a ball, pat it into a disk, and wrap it tightly in plastic wrap. Refrigerate for 30 minutes.

3. Remove the dough from the refrigerator and unwrap. Divide the dough to make the portions you need and again pat gently into disks. On a lightly floured work surface, roll out each dough disk into a round about ¼ inch thick and about 1 inch greater in diameter than the pan you are using (8 inches for a 7-inch pan; 4 inches for 3½-inch tartlet pans). Drape the rolled-out dough into the tart pan(s), gently pushing

continued

baking after the filling has been added. For fillings that are completely cooked and cooled before being poured into the shell, you fully pre-bake the shell to golden doneness, then fill it and chill thoroughly to bind the flavors before serving.

it into the bottom edges and against the pan sides to make a strong and straight shell. Trim the edges flush with the rim of the pan(s) using a sharp knife, or roll the rolling pin over the edges to cut off the excess dough. Prick all over the bottom with the tines of a fork and place in the freezer to firm up for 30 minutes. (To store unbaked, wrap the dough ball tightly in plastic wrap and freeze for up to 2 months, or line the tart shell(s) with the dough as desired, cover with plastic wrap, and freeze for up to 3 days. Thaw the frozen dough ball in the refrigerator for 3 to 4 hours before rolling and shaping. Bake lined and frozen shells straight out of the freezer.)

4. Preheat the oven to 350 degrees F.

5. To partially pre-bake the tart shell(s), place in the oven directly from the freezer and bake just until no longer translucent, 5 to 8 minutes.

   To fully pre-bake the tart shell(s), bake until golden brown, about 10 minutes.

6. Transfer to a wire rack and let cool completely before filling and proceeding with the recipe. Store fully baked shells, wrapped tightly in plastic, at room temperature for up to 3 days.

CHOCOLATE TRUFFLE TART

makes one 7-inch tart

The chocolate tart, like the lemon tart, is a staple in any patisserie. In creating a version of something that is so venerable, I believe you have two choices: to be radically innovative or strictly traditional. In the case of this chocolate tart, I chose the traditional route and relied on the simplicity of superb ingredients refining the proportions to take this out of the ordinary. The pâte sucrée once again demonstrates its ability to accentuate any filling, and the ganache is smooth and shiny like a truffle.

ingredients

ONE 7-INCH PÂTE SUCRÉE TART SHELL (PAGE 105)

ABOUT 1½ CUPS CHOCOLATE GANACHE (PAGE 195)

preparation

1. Make the Pâte Sucrée and line a 7-inch tart pan. Fully pre-bake the shell, transfer to a wire rack, and let cool completely.

2. Scoop the ganache into a microwave-safe bowl. (If the ganache was made earlier and has been chilled to a solid, first microwave on high for 1 minute to soften. Stir very gently so as not to agitate the chocolate, which would introduce air. Microwave at 10-second intervals, gently stirring between each, until the ganache is mostly liquid. Alternatively, soften over a bain-marie or double boiler.) Have ready an immersion blender, which you will use to make the glaze very smooth and pourable. Add about 2 tablespoons very hot water to the ganache, and let the water sit on top. Insert the head of the blender, while it is off, into the ganache very slowly at a 30-degree angle; you do not want to trap any air in the compartment of the head. When the head of the blender is submerged, twist the blender to a 90-degree angle and turn it on. Begin to make gentle circles, never up and down and never breaking the surface, until the chocolate is very shiny and smooth, 3 to 5 minutes. Be patient, as you will need more time than you think. When you begin to see a shine develop, you will think you are done, but go on a little longer. It should be very liquid at this point.

3. Pour the ganache into the tart shell. Refrigerate until well chilled, at least 1 hour and up to 8 hours, then remove from the refrigerator 30 minutes before serving.

continued

CHOCOLATE TRUFFLE TARTLETTES

1. Make the Pâte Sucrée and line ten 3½-inch tartlet pans. Fully pre-bake the shells, transfer to a wire rack, and let cool completely.

2. Pipe or spoon about ¼ cup ganache into each shell (you will need about 2 cups ganache total) and spread evenly. Chill for at least 1 hour or up to 8 hours, then remove from the refrigerator 30 minutes before serving. Makes ten 3½-inch tartlets.

Chocolate truffle tartlette

5

LIME MERINGUE TART

makes one 7-inch tart

This tart started with the combined desire to reinvent the refreshing flavor of Key lime pie and to find another use for our glorious Boiled Icing. Adding these to our home-made graham crust, the result was far from traditional and, in fact, represents the most innovative flavor combination at Miette.

Unlike traditional graham cracker crusts, which are made with cookie crumbs, the crust for this tart is made using the dough and baked off like a regular tart shell. You can make the lime cream and graham shells separately up to 2 or 3 days ahead, but make the boiled icing and fill the tart the day you will serve it. You will need a small blowtorch to caramelize the top of the meringue as we do at the bakery.

The recipe yields about 2 cups of lime cream, and you will use about 1 cup in a 7-inch tart or around 2 cups for 10 tartlets. Any leftover filling can be covered tightly and stored in the refrigerator for up to 1 week, or frozen for up 2 months.

ingredients

ONE 7-INCH GRAHAM CRACKER CRUST (PAGE 152)

LIME CREAM:

½ CUP FRESHLY SQUEEZED LIME JUICE

2 TABLESPOONS GRATED LIME ZEST

½ CUP PLUS 2 TABLESPOONS (4½ OUNCES) SUGAR

3 LARGE EGGS

¾ CUP PLUS 2 TABLESPOONS (7 OUNCES) UNSALTED BUTTER, CUBED

ABOUT 1 CUP BOILED ICING (PAGE 192)

preparation

1. Make the Graham Cracker Crust and line a 7-inch tart pan. Fully pre-bake the shell, transfer to a wire rack, and let cool completely.

2. To make the lime cream: In the top bowl of a double boiler or bain-marie, whisk together the lime juice, zest, sugar, and eggs. Fit the top bowl into the bottom pan over gently simmering water and warm the mixture, whisking occasionally, until it registers about 172 degrees F on an instant-read thermometer or coats the back of a wooden spoon and leaves a clear trail when a finger is drawn through it, 15 to 20 minutes.

3. Remove the mixture from the heat and strain through a fine-mesh sieve into a clean container. Let cool slightly, to about 140 degrees F, about 20 minutes.

continued

STEP 6a: Pipe the icing on top of the tart.

STEP 6b: Use the back of a spoon to press the icing to the edges of the crust.

STEP 6c: Brown the surface of the icing.

4. Add the butter to the cream mixture, a few cubes at a time, and, using a whisk or an immersion blender, blend until it dissolves completely after each addition. Strain the cream again to remove any lumps of butter, then let cool to room temperature. Place plastic wrap directly on the surface of the cream to prevent a skin from forming and refrigerate until well chilled, at least 2 hours and up to 3 days.

5. Prepare the Boiled Icing.

6. Spread the chilled lime cream into the cooled graham crust. Fit a pastry bag with a medium (½- or ⅝-inch) round tip and fill the bag about halfway with the icing. Pull up the cuff and twist it to seal and tighten the icing down into the cone. Purge the bag of air bubbles by squeezing the bag until there is a burst of air and icing sputters out of the bag. Pipe the icing on top of the tart, and then use the back of a spoon to press it down to meet the edges of the crust. Make a decorative swirl on top. Using a small kitchen torch, brown the surface of the icing, moving the flame in a circular motion to burn the ridges of the swirl until lightly browned. Refrigerate until well-chilled, at least 1 hour and up to 6 hours.

LIME MERINGUE TARTLETTES

1. Make the Graham Cracker Crust and line ten 3½-inch tartlet pans. Fully pre-bake, transfer to wire racks, and let cool completely.

2. Spoon about ¼ cup lime cream into each shell and spread evenly (you will need about 2 cups total of lime cream). Top with icing and torch as directed. Refrigerate until well-chilled, at least 1 hour and up to 6 hours. Makes ten 3½-inch tartlets.

LEMON TART

makes one 7-inch tart

The lemon tart is one of the quintessential French pastries, the simplicity of which belies its sophistication. A great lemon tart is a balance of flavors and textures; the play of sweet citrusy filling in a tender, crisp, buttery crust. In creating the version for Miette, I wanted to keep the traditional look of the straight-sided tart and fill it with a curd that was both fresh and rich. What I didn't realize when I started on my quest to make the best lemon tart was how easy it would be to make lemon curd with the year-round abundance of lemons we have locally, making this version quintessentially Californian.

The curd needs to be cold when assembling the tart, so make sure it is chilled before you begin. Likewise, once filled, it needs to chill to allow the crust and the filling to bind, but the tart is best served at room temperature.

Both components can be made separately up to 2 days ahead. Wrap the baked shell in plastic wrap and store it for up to 3 days at room temperature. Keep the curd refrigerated and fill the tart on the day you will serve it.

ingredients

ONE 7-INCH PÂTE SUCRÉE TART SHELL (PAGE 105)

ABOUT 1½ CUPS LEMON CURD (PAGE 200), CHILLED

preparation

1. Make the Pâte Sucrée and line a 7-inch tart pan. Fully pre-bake the shell, transfer to a wire rack, and let cool completely.

2. Spread the cold curd evenly into the cooled tart shell. Refrigerate until well chilled, at least 1 hour and up to 6 hours.

LEMON TARTLETTES

1. Make the Pâte Sucrée and line ten 3½-inch tartlet pans. Fully pre-bake, transfer to wire racks, and let cool completely.

2. Spoon about ¼ cup of the curd into each shell (you will need about 2 cups curd total) and spread evenly. Refrigerate until well chilled, at least 1 hour and up to 6 hours. Makes about ten 3½-inch tartlets.

PASTRY CREAM AND FRESH FRUIT TART

makes one 7-inch tart

I have yet to meet a fruit that doesn't pair deliciously with pâte sucrée and pastry cream. Sometimes I think we should just sell tart shells with pastry cream and let our customers add whatever fruit they want from the farmers' market. At Miette, we create variations all summer long, beginning with the too-short season of blueberries and ending with raspberries. One of our favorite variations is to pair raspberries and pastry cream flavored with rose geranium essential oil (see Sources, page 218). You could also add slices of nectarines and peaches in a single layer across the tart. Plush apricots and figs pair well, too, halved and nestled in the cream. Choose the ripest, most gorgeous fruit you can find.

ingredients

ABOUT 1½ CUPS PASTRY CREAM (PAGE 202), CHILLED

ONE 7-INCH PÂTE SUCRÉE TART SHELL (PAGE 105)

1 TO 2 PINTS MIXED FRESH FRUITS ALONE OR IN ANY COMBINATION INCLUDING STRAWBERRIES, BLUEBERRIES, BLACKBERRIES, AND RED AND GOLDEN RASPBERRIES; OR 2 OR 3 PEELED AND THINLY SLICED NECTARINES AND PEACHES; OR 10 TO 12 HALVED APRICOTS OR FIGS

preparation

1. If making the Pastry Cream now, let cool to room temperature and then refrigerate until well chilled, 2 to 3 hours.

2. Make the Pâte Sucrée and line a 7-inch tart pan as directed. Fully prebake the shell, transfer to a wire rack, and let cool completely.

3. Spread the cold pastry cream evenly into the cooled tart shell. Chill for at least 1 hour and up to 8 hours. Just before serving, top attractively with the fruit.

continued

PASTRY CREAM AND
FRESH FRUIT TARTLETTES

1. Make the Pâte Sucrée and line ten 3½-inch tartlet pans. Fully pre-bake, transfer to wire racks, and let cool completely.

2. Spoon about 2½ tablespoons of the pastry cream into each shell and spread evenly. Refrigerate until well chilled, at least 1 hour and up to 8 hours. Just before serving, top attractively with the fruit. Makes ten 3½-inch tartlets.

BANANA CREAM TART

makes one 7-inch tart

This familiar American classic can be found in diners across the country and tends to rely on the same basic ingredients. Our version refines the flavors by using high-quality ingredients and adds a buttery new dimension with the pâte sucrée crust and a depth of flavor with our chocolate ganache. Use bananas that are perfectly ripe for both flavor and texture, and cut them right before putting the tart together. You can prepare the crust and the ganache ahead of time and then top with the bananas and whipped cream just before serving, or refrigerate for up to 8 hours.

¾ CUP PASTRY CREAM (PAGE 202), CHILLED

ONE 7-INCH PÂTE SUCRÉE TART SHELL (PAGE 105)

¼ CUP CHOCOLATE GANACHE (PAGE 195)

2 LARGE RIPE BANANAS

1 CUP HEAVY CREAM

3 TABLESPOONS POWDERED SUGAR

¼ CUP (14 OUNCES) CHOCOLATE SHAVINGS

preparation

1. If making the Pastry Cream now, let cool to room temperature, and then refrigerate until well chilled, 2 to 3 hours.

2. Make the Pâte Sucrée and line a 7-inch tart pan as directed. Fully prebake the shell, transfer to a wire rack, and let cool completely.

3. If you made the ganache previously, scoop into a microwave-safe bowl and microwave on high for 1 minute to warm and soften until the mixture is easily spreadable. Alternatively, soften over a bain-marie or double boiler (see page 215).

4. Spread the ganache onto the bottom surface of the cooled pastry shell. Refrigerate until set, about 10 minutes.

5. Cut the bananas into slices about ⅛ inch thick. Working quickly, arrange in a single layer over the ganache. Immediately spread the pastry cream over the bananas. Smooth the surface with an offset spatula.

6. In a chilled bowl, using an electric mixer set on high speed, whip the heavy cream until soft peaks form. Add the powdered sugar and continue to whip until the cream stands in stiff peaks.

7. Fit a pastry bag with a medium (½- or ⅝-inch) star tip and fill it halfway with the whipped cream. Pull up the cuff and twist it to seal and tighten the whipped cream down into the cone. Purge the bag of air bubbles by squeezing the bag until there is a burst of air and whipped cream sputters out of the bag. Keep the bag tightly twisted so that the whipped cream doesn't come back up on your hands. Holding the bag at a 90-degree angle and using focused little bursts of pressure, pipe small stars all over the surface of the pastry cream, working in a spiral motion toward the center to make a charming constellation. Sprinkle the surface with the chocolate shavings.

8. The tart is best served right away, but will keep, tightly wrapped in the refrigerator, for up to 8 hours.

BANANA CREAM TARTLETTES

1. Make the Pâte Sucrée and line ten 3½-inch tartlet pans. Fully pre-bake, transfer to a wire rack, and let cool completely.

2. Pipe or spoon about 2 tablespoons of the ganache into each shell and spread evenly. Arrange banana slices over the ganache. Immediately spoon and spread about 2 tablespoons of pastry cream over the bananas in each tartlet. Smooth the surface with an offset spatula.

3. Fill a pastry bag with whipped cream and, using focused little bursts of pressure, pipe a triple rosette of cream on each tartlet. Sprinkle the surface with the chocolate shavings. Serve immediately, or refrigerate for up to 8 hours. Makes ten 3½-inch tartlets.

PECAN TART

makes one 7-inch tart

In San Francisco, our Indian summer begins in September. After months of cold and fog, the weather is so warm that it's easy to forget that fall has arrived. It is more noticeably marked by the arrival of the Pecan Tart. This tart has a silky buttery filling, a deep caramel flavor, and a hint of orange that define it against most traditional pecan pies. Toasting the nuts first is crucial in creating that satisfying taste, as is baking the tart fully to a dark amber color.

ingredients

ONE 7-INCH PÂTE SUCRÉE TART SHELL (PAGE 105)

1 CUP (4 OUNCES) PECAN HALVES

¾ CUP LIGHT CORN SYRUP

¾ CUP (6 OUNCES) FIRMLY PACKED LIGHT BROWN SUGAR

¼ CUP (2 OUNCES) UNSALTED BUTTER, MELTED

2 LARGE EGGS

2 TABLESPOONS HEAVY CREAM

1 TEASPOON GRATED ORANGE ZEST

⅛ TEASPOON KOSHER SALT

½ TEASPOON VANILLA EXTRACT

preparation

1. Make the Pâte Sucrée and line a 7-inch tart pan. Partially pre-bake the shell, transfer to a wire rack, and let cool completely on the baking sheet.

2. Preheat the oven to 350 degrees F.

3. Spread the pecans in single layer on a baking sheet and toast in the oven until browned and fragrant, 8 to 10 minutes. Remove from the oven and immediately pour onto a plate to prevent scorching.

4. In a medium bowl, whisk together the corn syrup, brown sugar, melted butter, eggs, cream, orange zest, salt, and vanilla until smooth. Arrange the pecans on the bottom of the pastry shell in an attractive manner. Pour the filling slowly on top of the pecans until it almost reaches the top edge of the crust.

5. Carefully slide the baking sheet with the tart into the oven. Bake until the juices are bubbling and the filling is set, 25 to 30 minutes. Transfer to a wire rack and let cool completely before serving. Serve at room temperature.

PECAN TARTLETTES

1. Make the Pâte Sucrée and line ten 3½-inch tartlet pans. Partially pre-bake the shells, transfer to a wire rack, and let cool completely.

2. Add a single layer of pecans to the bottom of each shell. Spoon about ¼ cup of the filling into each tartlet. Bake until the juices are bubbling and the filling is firm, about 20 minutes. Transfer to a wire rack and let cool completely before serving. Serve at room temperature. Makes ten 3½-inch tartlets.

Graham crackers
$6.50

cookies, bars, and pastries

COOKIES, BARS, AND PASTRIES

As you approach our shop in the Ferry Building, you see a green table tiered with cookies in their polka-dot bags. There have been a few customer "favorites" over the years. The first was the Chocolate Sablé, a tribute to Pierre Hermé, with its flakes of 62 percent cacao chocolate in the dough. Then came the Graham Cracker, a snappy reinvention of the classic. And now everything lives in the shadow of the Gingersnap. And although it has never been a contender, the Peanut Butter Cookie is the bag I take home. Also in this chapter are our signature Eclairs, as well as our Crème Fraîche Scones and brownies.

In a category all its own, the macaron has a long celebrated history in France but was virtually unknown in the United States when we started to make them. Not to be confused with the coconut macaroon, our macaron consists of two meringue-almond cookies sandwiched with buttercream or ganache, which we make with organic ingredients in an array of natural flavors. It's now one of our most sought-after creations.

Whereas a cake stands on ceremony, cookies are the little everyday indulgences: crispy, buttery, sometimes salty, and filled with nuts. Although relatively easy to make, a great cookie is nothing less than exquisite. And because there is so little technique, their success lies directly in the ingredients you use. Once again, find the best butter available, toast your nuts, and handle the dough with care.

Because our cookies are small, some of the recipe yields are quite large. Wrap extra cookies in cello bags and give them away to your friends or store in airtight containers for up to 2 weeks.

CHOCOLATE WAFER COOKIES

makes about twenty-four 3¼-inch cookies

I wanted to re-create the chocolate wafer cookie that is used to make the famous Icebox Cake—a cake made with layers of cookies and whipped cream and put in the refrigerator until set. The Miette version is crisp, chocolatey, and salty-sweet right at the end. We use brut cocoa powder, a type that is especially dark and makes the cookie really black (see Sources, page 218). Regular cocoa powder will impart the same taste even though the color will be lighter. You can store extra dough in the freezer for up to 2 months.

1¾ CUPS (9 OUNCES) ALL-PURPOSE FLOUR

½ CUP PLUS 2 TABLESPOONS (2 OUNCES) BRUT OR NATURAL UNSWEETENED COCOA POWDER (SEE NOTE, PAGE 57)

¼ TEASPOON KOSHER SALT

1 CUP (8 OUNCES) UNSALTED BUTTER, AT ROOM TEMPERATURE

½ CUP (3½ OUNCES) GRANULATED SUGAR, PLUS EXTRA FOR SPRINKLING

2 TABLESPOONS LIGHTLY PACKED LIGHT BROWN SUGAR

3 TABLESPOONS HONEY

preparation

1. Sift together the flour, cocoa powder, and salt into a bowl. Set aside.

2. In the bowl of a stand mixer fitted with the paddle attachment, combine the butter, granulated and brown sugars, and honey and beat until fluffy, about 4 minutes.

3. Add the dry ingredients to the butter mixture in three additions, beating just until combined after each. Wrap the dough tightly in plastic wrap and refrigerate for at least 30 minutes or for up to 2 days. You can also freeze the dough for up to 2 months.

4. Preheat the oven to 350 degrees F. Line a large baking sheet with parchment paper.

continued

5. Unwrap the dough. On a lightly floured work surface, roll out to about ¼ inch thick. Using a 3¼-inch round cookie cutter with a scalloped edge, cut out the chocolate wafers. Arrange on the prepared baking sheet, placing the cookies about ½ inch apart. Sprinkle each cookie with granulated sugar. Bake until firm, 12 to 15 minutes. Transfer to a wire rack to cool completely. They should snap crisply when cooled.

6. Gather up the dough scraps, reroll, and cut out to make more cookies. Bake as directed and let cool. Store in an airtight container for up to 2 weeks.

CHOCOLATE WAFER CRUMBS

Place the baked and cooled cookies in a food processor and pulse to fine crumbs in 5-second intervals, until the texture of coarse sand, 3 or 4 times. Store in an airtight container for up to 2 weeks. Makes about 4 cups crumbs.

THUMBPRINT COOKIES

makes about thirty-six 2-inch cookies

A favorite with children, these thumb-prints are tender butter cookies filled with jam. In the bakery, the flavor of the jam is left undecided until we select our fruit at the market. The red fruits, such as raspberry and strawberry, make beautiful jewel-toned centers and contrast nicely with the golden color of the cookie. My favorite version of this cookie uses huckleberry jam; I like how the tartness of the berries contrasts and complements the sweet, salty, buttery cookie. Use a seedless jam that has enough body to keep its shape. Or, if your favorite jam has seeds, strain them out by heating the jam slightly and passing it through a sieve.

ingredients

1½ CUPS (7½ OUNCES) ALL-PURPOSE FLOUR

¼ TEASPOON BAKING POWDER

¼ TEASPOON KOSHER SALT

¾ CUP (6 OUNCES) UNSALTED BUTTER, AT ROOM TEMPERATURE

½ CUP (4 OUNCES) SUGAR

2 TEASPOONS VANILLA EXTRACT

¼ TEASPOON ALMOND EXTRACT

1 LARGE EGG

ABOUT ½ CUP (6 OUNCES) SEEDLESS FRUIT JAM

preparation

1. Sift together the flour, baking powder, and salt into a small bowl. Set aside.

2. In the bowl of a stand mixer fitted with the paddle attachment, beat together the butter, sugar, vanilla, and almond extract on medium speed until pale and fluffy, about 5 minutes. Stop the mixer and scrape down the sides of the bowl with a rubber spatula. Add the egg and beat on medium speed just until combined.

3. Add the dry ingredients to the butter mixture on low speed until just combined. Form the dough into a disk and wrap in plastic wrap. Refrigerate for at least 1 hour or up to 2 days to firm the dough.

4. Preheat the oven to 350 degrees F. Line two large baking sheets with parchment paper.

5. Use a teaspoon to scoop up rounds of dough and shape them into balls about the size of a shooter marble. It's better for the balls to be taller rather than wider. Place them 2 inches apart on the prepared baking sheets. Bake until lightly browned, 12 to 14 minutes. Immediately use the round end of a wooden spoon or other implement to make an indentation in the center of each warm cookie. Immediately fill each hole with about ¼ teaspoon jam. You can heat the jam slightly to make this process easier. Either spoon it in or put the jam in a small pastry bag and quickly pipe it into the depressions.

6. Transfer the cookies to a wire rack to cool. Leave the cookies at room temperature to allow the jam to set, about 30 minutes. Store in airtight containers for up to 2 weeks.

CHOCOLATE CHIP COOKIES

makes about thirty-six 5-inch cookies and one hundred twenty 2-inch cookies

There is much debate about what makes the perfect chocolate chip cookie. Once I realized I would never make everyone happy, I created a version that exemplified my favorite cookie characteristics: small, crisp, buttery, crunchy. The ground oats and walnuts give the cookie its delightful crumbly texture.

While many bakeries make an oversized chocolate chip cookie, the Miette cookie is defiantly small. You'll need mini chocolate chips, which can be found in many grocery stores. We couldn't scale the recipe to make fewer, so this recipe makes ten dozen small Miette-sized cookies and three dozen "normal" 5-inch cookies.

ingredients

2 CUPS (10 OUNCES) ALL-PURPOSE FLOUR

1¼ TEASPOONS BAKING SODA

1 TEASPOON BAKING POWDER

¼ TEASPOON KOSHER SALT

1⅔ CUPS (7½ OUNCES) ROLLED OATS

¾ CUP (3½ OUNCES) WALNUTS, TOASTED AND COOLED

1 CUP (8 OUNCES) UNSALTED BUTTER, AT ROOM TEMPERATURE

1⅓ CUPS (10 OUNCES) SUGAR

1 LARGE EGG

1½ TABLESPOONS MILK

2½ TEASPOONS VANILLA EXTRACT

2 CUPS (12 OUNCES) SEMISWEET MINI CHOCOLATE CHIPS

preparation

1. Line two baking sheets with parchment paper.

2. Preheat the oven to 350 degrees F.

3. Sift together the flour, baking soda, baking powder, and salt into a bowl. Set aside.

4. In a food processor, process the oats to coarse crumbs. Transfer to a plate, then add the walnuts to the food processor and pulse just until coarsely ground, in 5-second pulses, three or four times. Do not over-mix or the nuts will get buttery. Set aside.

continued

5. In the bowl of a stand mixer fitted with the paddle attachment, combine the butter and sugar and beat on high speed until the mixture is light-colored and fluffy, about 5 minutes. Stop the mixer and scrape down the sides of the bowl with a rubber spatula, then add the egg and beat until thoroughly incorporated. Add the milk and vanilla and beat to mix well. Add the sifted dry ingredients and beat until just combined. Scrape down the sides of the bowl again. Remove the bowl from the mixer. Add the oats, chocolate chips, and walnuts and stir by hand just until the ingredients are evenly distributed.

6. To make the small cookies, roll scant teaspoon-size portions of dough into ¾-inch balls. To make the larger cookies, roll the dough into 2-inch balls. Place them about 2 inches apart on the prepared baking sheets, and, using the palm of your hand, flatten each dough ball slightly. Bake in batches until lightly browned, about 10 minutes. Remove the cookies to a wire rack to cool completely. Store in airtight containers for up to 2 weeks.

PEANUT BUTTER COOKIES

makes about twenty-four 2½-inch cookies or one hundred twenty 1½-inch cookies

Our first bakery location was in an old flour mill that also made a variety of nut butters and pastes, including the peanut butter for these cookies. Unlike most peanut butter cookies, which tend to be soft, these cookies are crisp and melt in your mouth with a shortbread-like texture. If you can, freshly grind your own peanut butter with a coarse setting, leaving a few big peanut pieces for extra crunch. We use a meat mallet to cross-hatch our cookies (see next page).

1½ CUPS (7½ OUNCES) ALL-PURPOSE FLOUR

1 TEASPOON BAKING SODA

¼ TEASPOON KOSHER SALT

½ CUP (4 OUNCES) UNSALTED BUTTER, SOFTENED

½ CUP (4 OUNCES) GRANULATED SUGAR, PLUS MORE FOR SPRINKLING

⅓ CUP (2½ OUNCES) PACKED LIGHT BROWN SUGAR

½ TEASPOON VANILLA EXTRACT

1 LARGE EGG

½ CUP PLUS 2 TABLESPOONS (5½ OUNCES) CREAMY OR CHUNKY PEANUT BUTTER

preparation

1. Line two baking sheets with parchment paper. Preheat the oven to 350 degrees F.

2. Sift together the flour, baking soda, and salt into a bowl. Set aside.

3. In the bowl of a stand mixer fitted with the paddle attachment, on high speed, beat together the butter, granulated and brown sugars, and vanilla until light and fluffy, 4 to 5 minutes. Add the egg and beat until incorporated. Scrape down the sides of the bowl with a rubber spatula. Add the peanut butter and mix until smooth and uniform.

continued

4. Add the dry ingredients and mix until just combined. Remove the bowl from the mixer, scrape down the sides of the bowl, and mix again a few times by hand.

5. To make the small cookies, roll scant 1-teaspoon portions of dough into ¾-inch balls. To make the larger cookies, roll 1½-tablespoon portions of dough into balls. Place them 2 inches apart on the prepared baking sheets. Flatten slightly and imprint the traditional cross-hatch marks using the back of a fork or a meat mallet. Sprinkle with granulated sugar. Bake in batches until lightly browned, about 10 minutes. Remove the cookies to a wire rack to cool completely. Store in airtight containers for up to 2 weeks.

LEMON SHORTBREAD COOKIES

makes about forty-eight 1¼-inch cookies

On a recent trip to Scotland, I ate my body weight in shortbread. The Scots are known as the originators of shortbread and I was seeking out any new bits of knowledge that could perfect the Miette version. It turns out the perfection of this cookie lies not in a secret ingredient, but in quality ingredients.

This lemon shortbread recipe takes the tart, fresh flavor of lemons and contrasts it beautifully with the richness of butter. In the walnut version (page 138), the nuts add a wonderful earthy taste that we accentuate with sea salt.

It is important to stop mixing just at the point when the dough clumps together. This prevents the cookies from becoming tough. Freezing the dough makes the cookies more crumbly and helps them maintain their shape while baking. Don't underbake these cookies. They should be golden brown.

ingredients

⅔ CUP (5 OUNCES) SUGAR, PLUS MORE FOR SPRINKLING

2 TABLESPOONS GRATED LEMON ZEST

2 CUPS (8 OUNCES) ALL-PURPOSE FLOUR

1 CUP (8 OUNCES) COLD UNSALTED BUTTER, CUBED

½ TEASPOON KOSHER SALT

¼ TEASPOON BAKING SODA

6 TABLESPOONS HEAVY CREAM

1 TEASPOON VANILLA EXTRACT

preparation

1. Using a mortar and pestle or clean spice grinder, grind together the sugar and lemon zest.

2. In the bowl of a stand mixer fitted with the paddle attachment, combine the flour, butter, salt, and baking soda and beat on low speed until it resembles cornmeal. Add the lemon sugar, cream, and vanilla and beat until just clumped together.

3. If the dough is soft, wrap it tightly in plastic wrap and refrigerate for 30 minutes. Otherwise, roll out the dough ½ inch thick on a lightly floured surface into a 6-by-4-inch rectangle. Using a ruler, square the edges as much as possible. Using a sharp knife or pizza cutter, cut the dough into 1-inch squares. Place them 2 inches apart on a parchment-lined baking sheet. Sprinkle lightly with sugar.

4. Preheat the oven to 350 degrees F. Bake the cookies until they are golden brown, 10 to 12 minutes. Remove to a wire rack to cool. Store in airtight containers for up to 2 weeks.

WALNUT SHORTBREAD COOKIES

makes about forty-eight 1¼-inch cookies

The toasted flavor of walnuts heightens the buttery quality of shortbread. The additional fat in the nuts necessitated different proportions than in our lemon version (see page 137), hence this recipe.

ingredients

½ CUP (2 OUNCES) WALNUT PIECES

1¾ CUPS (9 OUNCES) ALL-PURPOSE FLOUR

½ TEASPOON KOSHER SALT

1 CUP (8 OUNCES) COLD UNSALTED BUTTER, CUBED

¾ CUP (5½ OUNCES) SUGAR

1 EGG YOLK

MALDON SEA SALT

preparation

1. Preheat the oven to 350 degrees F.

2. Toast the walnuts until lightly browned, 12 to 15 minutes. Let cool, then finely grind them in a food processor.

3. Sift together the flour and salt into a bowl and set aside. In the bowl of a stand mixer fitted with a paddle attachment on low speed, beat together the butter and sugar until lightened, about 4 minutes. Add the egg yolk and mix until fully incorporated. Add the dry ingredients and walnuts and mix just to combine.

4. If the dough is soft, wrap it tightly in plastic wrap and refrigerate for 30 minutes. Otherwise, roll out the dough ½ inch thick on a lightly floured work surface into a 6-by-7-inch rectangle. Using a ruler, square the edges as much as possible. Using a sharp knife or pizza cutter, cut the dough into 1-inch squares. Place them about 2 inches apart on a parchment-lined baking sheet. Sprinkle lightly with sea salt.

5. Bake the cookies until they are firm, 10 to 12 minutes. Remove to a wire rack to cool. Store in airtight containers for up to 2 weeks.

CHOCOLATE SABLÉS

makes about thirty-six 1-inch square cookies

If ever you are in Paris, you must make a visit to the Pierre Hermé boutique on rue Bonaparte. I made such a pilgrimage during a trip the first year I was in business, joining the queue that wraps around the block. As I inched into the store, I filled my basket with one of everything off the shelf, including a canister of his chocolate sablés—the inspiration for this cookie. The Miette version replicates the same experience of biting into a crisp lattice supporting bits of pure, soft chocolate. Like our Double Chocolate Cake (page 55), this recipe calls for both cocoa and chocolate. When you bring these two ingredients together, you get a resounding chocolate taste, much more complex than if you were to use just one or the other. Use a high-quality chocolate and feel free to venture into something more bitter-sweet. The sprinkling of sugar on top can carry the intensity of a dark chocolate.

ingredients

1 CUP (5 OUNCES) ALL-PURPOSE FLOUR

⅓ CUP (1 OUNCE) NATURAL UNSWEETENED COCOA POWDER (SEE NOTE, PAGE 57)

½ TEASPOON BAKING SODA

½ CUP (4 OUNCES) UNSALTED BUTTER, AT ROOM TEMPERATURE

⅔ CUP (4½ OUNCES) SUGAR, PLUS MORE FOR SPRINKLING

¼ TEASPOON SEA SALT

¾ TEASPOON VANILLA EXTRACT

3½ OUNCES 70 PERCENT CACAO CHOCOLATE, GRATED

preparation

1. Sift together the flour, cocoa powder, and baking soda into a bowl and set aside.

2. In the bowl of a stand mixer fitted with the paddle attachment, beat together the butter, sugar, salt, and vanilla until lightened, about 4 minutes. Add the dry ingredients and grated chocolate and mix just to combine.

3. If the dough is soft, wrap it tightly in plastic wrap and refrigerate for 30 minutes. (The dough will keep, wrapped in plastic, for up to 1 week in the refrigerator or 3 months in the freezer.) Otherwise, roll out the dough ½ inch thick on a lightly floured work surface into a 6-by-7-inch rectangle. Using a ruler, square the edges as much as possible. Using a sharp knife or pizza cutter, cut the dough into 1-inch squares. Place them 2 inches apart on a parchment-lined baking sheet. Sprinkle lightly with sugar.

4. Preheat the oven to 350 degrees F. Bake the cookies until they are firm, 10 to 12 minutes. Remove to a wire rack to cool. Store in airtight containers for up to 2 weeks.

GINGERSNAPS

makes about twenty-four 3¼-inch cookies

We use three forms of ginger in this recipe to give the cookies spiciness, earthiness, and a little heat. The cookies are crisp and should literally snap; don't underbake them or they will be too soft. What makes this gingersnap different from others is the large proportion of butter; it is as much a butter cookie as it is a ginger cookie. We package these in clear canisters to show off their pretty scalloped edges.

2 CUPS (10 OUNCES) ALL-PURPOSE FLOUR

½ CUP (2½ OUNCES) WHOLE-WHEAT FLOUR

½ TEASPOON KOSHER SALT

2 TABLESPOONS PLUS 1 TEASPOON GROUND GINGER

GENEROUS ¼ TEASPOON GROUND CINNAMON

⅛ TEASPOON GROUND CLOVES

⅛ TEASPOON GROUND WHITE PEPPER

⅛ TEASPOON GROUND NUTMEG

SCANT ⅛ TEASPOON GROUND CARDAMOM

1 CUP (8 OUNCES) UNSALTED BUTTER, AT ROOM TEMPERATURE

¾ CUP (5 OUNCES) LIGHTLY PACKED LIGHT BROWN SUGAR

2 TABLESPOONS HONEY

4 TABLESPOONS MOLASSES

½ CUP (2 OUNCES) FINELY MINCED CANDIED GINGER

2 TEASPOONS FRESH GINGER PURÉE (GRATED WITH A MICROPLANE), OR PURCHASED GINGER PURÉE (SEE SOURCES, PAGE 218)

GRANULATED SUGAR FOR SPRINKLING

1. Sift together both flours, the salt, and spices into a bowl. Set aside.

2. In the bowl of a stand mixer fitted with the paddle attachment on low speed, beat together the butter and sugar until fluffy, 4 to 5 minutes. Add the honey and molasses and mix until fully incorporated.

3. Add the dry ingredients to the butter mixture in three additions, mixing just to combine after each addition. Mix in the candied ginger and ginger purée until just combined. Form the dough into a disk, wrap tightly in plastic wrap and refrigerate for at least 30 minutes or up to 2 days before rolling.

4. Preheat the oven to 350 degrees F. Line two baking sheets with parchment paper.

5. Roll the dough on a lightly floured surface to about ¼ inch thick. Cut with a scalloped 3¼-inch round cutter and place on the baking sheets ½ inch apart. Sprinkle each cookie with granulated sugar. Bake until deeply browned, 10 to 12 minutes. Remove to a wire rack to cool. Store in airtight containers for up to 2 weeks.

PARISIAN MACARONS

makes eighteen 1-inch sandwich cookies

This unusual and delicious little cookie transformed Miette. Although they have been extremely popular in France for decades, macarons didn't catch my interest until a trip to Paris in our first year of business. We started experimenting with a recipe as soon as we returned, but found very little information to guide us toward reliable results. In lieu of any guidelines, we created a version that is distinctly ours with coarsely ground organic almonds and natural flavors and colors. They were an eyesore to anyone used to seeing the perfectly smooth, vividly colored originals. But within a year, we were getting visitors from all over the world just for the macarons. Now, more than half of our bakery staff is focused on the production of these dense, chewy, and meltingly light sandwich cookies.

Although there are only four ingredients, there are an infinite number of ways to go wrong. Macarons are mysterious, and factors including humidity, oven temperature, and the quality of your egg whites may have an effect. Just do your best and make adjustments if

continued

ingredients

1½ CUPS (7½ OUNCES) WHOLE ALMONDS, WITH SKINS

2¼ CUPS (10 OUNCES) POWDERED SUGAR

3 LARGE EGG WHITES = 1/2 cup

1½ TEASPOONS CREAM OF TARTAR

1½ CUPS VANILLA BUTTERCREAM (PAGE 185) OR CHOCOLATE GANACHE (PAGE 195), PREPARED FOR SPREADING

preparation

1. Line two large baking sheets with parchment paper. Using a 1½-inch bottle cap as a template, draw 1-inch circles in rows on the paper, about 1 inch apart. You should have room for eighteen circles on each sheet.

2. Place half of the almonds and half of the powdered sugar in a food processor. Process for 30 seconds, until the almonds are finely ground. Pour the mixture into a separate bowl, and repeat the process with the remaining almonds and powdered sugar. Set aside.

3. In the bowl of a stand mixer fitted with the whisk attachment, combine the egg whites and cream of tartar and whisk on high speed until very stiff peaks form, 3 to 4 minutes.

4. Using a rubber spatula, gently fold about one-third of the almond mixture into the egg whites. Fold in the remaining mixture in two more additions, just until the ingredients are completely combined.

continued

STEP 5:   Pipe 1-inch circles, ½ to ¾ inch high.

STEP 7:   Top half of the cookies with a nickel-size dollop of filling.

necessary. Crucial to our macarons are almonds that we grind ourselves. Although it is a tricky step, because you need to make sure you don't overgrind and end up with a clumpy nut butter. To properly grind almonds, use a spice grinder and pulse raw almonds at 5-second intervals four or five times, until the consistency is a sandy, flecked, granular powder but not a paste. You can use commercially ground almonds, too, but you may end up with a macaron with a different texture.

At Miette, we make ten kinds of macarons, all included here. The plain macaron cookie is the base for the Vanilla, Lemon, Grapefruit, and Rose Geranium flavors. The Pistachio, Coffee, Hazelnut, Chocolate, and Chocolate-Orange versions each put a twist in the basic macaron recipe. The fillings are listed with each variation. Note that the cookies rest at room temperature for 2 hours before baking, a step that is crucial to achieving just the right balance of crispness and chewiness, so plan ahead. And if you choose to do the lemon macarons, you will have to make the lemon curd for the buttercream in advance.

5. Fit a pastry bag with a medium (½- or ⅝-inch) round tip and fill the bag with the meringue. Pull up the cuff and twist it to seal and tighten the meringue down into the cone. Purge the bag of air bubbles by squeezing the bag until there is a burst of air and meringue sputters out of the bag. Keep the bag tightly twisted so that the meringue doesn't come back up on your hands. Using the template as a guide, pipe 1-inch circles, ½ to ¾ inch high, onto the baking sheets. Set the baking sheets aside in a protected area and let the cookies stand at room temperature for 2 hours. This allows the macarons to develop their distinctive crust and a "foot" or base on the bottom.

6. Preheat the oven to 325 degrees F.

7. Bake the macarons until set but not browned, 10 to 12 minutes. Transfer the baking sheets to wire racks and let the macarons cool completely on the pans. When they are cool, use your fingers to carefully lift half of the cookies from the parchment and turn them upside down. Using a pastry bag fitted with a medium (½- or ⅝-inch) round tip and filled with either the buttercream or ganache, squeeze a nickle-size dollop of filling onto each of the upside-down cookies, and then top with the remaining macarons to complete the sandwich cookies.

8. Store the macarons in airtight containers for up to 2 weeks.

LEMON, GRAPEFRUIT, AND ROSE GERANIUM MACARONS

Make the Parisian Macarons and fill with Lemon Buttercream, Grapefruit Buttercream, or Rose Geranium Buttercream (pages 186–187), respectively.

continued

PISTACHIO MACARONS

Make the Parisian Macarons and reduce the amount of almonds to 1 cup (5 ounces) and add ⅓ cup (1½ ounces) unsalted whole pistachios. Sandwich with Pistachio Buttercream (page 186).

COFFEE MACARONS

Make the Parisian Macarons and sprinkle in 1½ teaspoons freeze-dried instant espresso powder with the first addition of sugar and almonds. Sandwich with Chocolate-Coffee Ganache (page 196).

HAZELNUT MACARONS

Reduce the amount of almonds to 1 cup (5 ounces) and add ⅓ cup (1½ ounces) whole hazelnuts, skins removed. Sandwich with Chocolate-Hazelnut Ganache (page 196).

CHOCOLATE MACARONS

Add ⅓ cup (1 ounce) natural unsweetened cocoa powder with the sugar. Omit the cream of tartar from the recipe as it will react with the cocoa powder. Sandwich with Chocolate Ganache (page 195).

CHOCOLATE-ORANGE MACARONS

Make the Chocolate Macarons (above). Sandwich with Chocolate-Orange Ganache (page 196).

GRAHAM CRACKERS

makes about twenty-four 3¼-inch cookies, two 7-inch tart shells, or twelve 3½-inch tartlette shells

We created this graham dough for the Lime Meringue Tart (page 111), but when we rolled it out a little thinner and punched cookie shapes, we discovered a superior version of this classic American cookie.

Graham is a type of whole-wheat flour that tends to have a coarse, uneven texture, so we don't use it. Instead, we make our dough using regular whole-wheat flour to produce a smooth, crisp, buttery cookie, flavored with a touch of honey.

This dough might be the most versatile in the bakery. The Miette Cheesecake (page 79) calls for these cookie crumbs in its crust. The Lime Meringue Tart calls for the dough to be rolled out (like a tart dough) and pressed into the pan before baking.

You can wrap extra dough in plastic wrap and freeze for up to 2 months. Defrost at room temperature.

ingredients

1½ CUPS (7½ OUNCES) ALL-PURPOSE FLOUR

⅓ CUP (1½ OUNCES) WHOLE-WHEAT FLOUR

½ TEASPOON KOSHER SALT

GENEROUS ¼ TEASPOON GROUND CINNAMON

⅔ CUP (6 OUNCES) UNSALTED BUTTER, AT ROOM TEMPERATURE

½ CUP (4 OUNCES) FIRMLY PACKED LIGHT BROWN SUGAR

2 TABLESPOONS HONEY

preparation

1. Sift together both flours, the salt, and cinnamon into a bowl. Set aside.

2. In the bowl of a stand mixer fitted with the paddle attachment, combine the butter, brown sugar, and honey and beat until fluffy, about 5 minutes.

3. Add the dry ingredients to the butter mixture in three additions, beating just until combined after each addition. Wrap the dough tightly in plastic wrap and refrigerate for at least 30 minutes before rolling, or for up to 2 days.

4. Preheat the oven to 350 degrees F. Line a large baking sheet with parchment paper.

continued

5. Unwrap the dough and place between two sheets of waxed paper. On a clean work surface, roll out to a thickness of about ¼ inch. Using a 3¼-inch round cookie cutter with a scalloped edge, cut out the graham crackers. Arrange on the prepared baking sheet, placing the cookies about ½ inch apart. Bake until golden brown, 10 to 12 minutes. Transfer to a wire rack and let cool completely. They should snap crisply when cooled.

6. Gather up the dough scraps, reroll, and cut out to make more cookies. Bake as directed and let cool. Store in an airtight container for up to 2 weeks.

GRAHAM CRACKER CRUMBS

To make enough crumbs for the cheesecake, place 12 of the baked and cooled graham crackers in a food processor and pulse at 5-second intervals until fine crumbs form, four to five times. Store in an airtight container for up to 2 weeks. Makes about 1½ cups crumbs.

GRAHAM CRACKER CRUST

1. Remove the dough from the refrigerator and unwrap. Divide the dough to make the portions you need (see recipe introduction) and again pat gently into disks. On a lightly floured work surface, roll out each dough disk into a round about ¼ inch thick and about 1 inch greater in diameter than the pan you are using (8 inches for a 7-inch pan; 4 inches for 3½-inch tartlet pans). Drape the rolled-out dough into the tart pan(s), gently pushing it into the bottom edges and against the pan sides to make a strong and straight shell. Trim the edges flush with the rim of the pan(s) using a sharp knife, or roll the rolling pin over the edges to cut off the excess dough. Prick all over the bottom with the tines of a fork and place in the freezer to firm up for 30 minutes.

2. Preheat the oven to 350 degrees F.

3. To fully blind-bake the shell, line the shells with parchment paper and weight with dried rice, dried beans, or pie weights. Place in the oven and bake until golden brown, about 10 minutes. Transfer to a wire rack and let cool completely before proceeding with the recipe.

BROWNIES

makes twelve brownie cupcakes or twenty-four 2-inch square brownies

Next to all of the fancy desserts in our case, the brownie looks quite humble until you taste it and realize how sublime a brownie can be: fudgey and cakey all at the same time. At Miette, we bake the brownies individually so that each gets crispy edges, which makes them even more delicious. The individual brownies make an elegant presentation. We use a special financier pan available to bakers (see Sources, page 218). Here, we give the option of using cupcake pans, or to use a 9-by-13 inch pan and cut the brownies to size, though these will not be quite to Miette style.

ingredients

1 CUP (4½ OUNCES) ALL-PURPOSE FLOUR

1 TEASPOON BAKING POWDER

¼ TEASPOON ESPRESSO POWDER

1 POUND 70 PERCENT CACAO CHOCOLATE, CHOPPED

2½ CUPS (18½ OUNCES) SUGAR

¾ CUP (6 OUNCES) UNSALTED BUTTER

1 TEASPOON VANILLA EXTRACT

½ TEASPOON KOSHER SALT

5 LARGE EGGS, WARMED IN A WATER BATH TO 80 TO 90 DEGREES F

1 CUP (3½ OUNCES) WALNUT HALVES (OPTIONAL)

preparation

1. Butter 12 standard cupcake cups or one 9-by-13-inch baking pan and dust with sifted cocoa. Tap out the excess cocoa.

2. Preheat the oven to 350 degrees F.

3. Sift together the flour, baking powder, and espresso powder into a bowl. Set aside.

4. In a large microwave-safe bowl, combine the chocolate, sugar, butter, vanilla, and salt. Microwave on high for 1 minute, then stir. Continue to microwave for 1-minute intervals until the chocolate is completely melted. (Alternatively, melt the chocolate in a double-boiler or bain-marie.)

continued

5. While still warm, transfer the chocolate mixture to the bowl of a stand mixer fitted with a paddle attachment. Mix on low for 30 seconds, then add the eggs, one at a time, beating after each addition until well combined and shiny. Add the flour mixture and beat just until combined. Raise the speed to medium and beat for another 30 seconds until the batter is shiny. It will be very liquid.

6. Scoop the batter into the prepared pan. If it is still warm, it should flow to the edges. If it has cooled, just use your offset spatula to smooth it into place. If using the walnuts, dot them on each cupcake or sprinkle them evenly over the pan and lightly press them into the batter. Bake the brownies until they begin to pull away from the sides of the pan and a tester inserted in the center comes out clean, 18 to 20 minutes for cupcakes or 40 to 45 minutes for the 9-by-13-inch pan.

7. Remove from the oven and immediately transfer the cupcakes from the pan to wire racks to cool. If using the baking pan, let the brownies cool in the pan for about 20 minutes, then cut them while still a tad warm into roughly 2-inch squares. Store in airtight containers for up to 1 week.

CRÈME FRAÎCHE SCONES

makes 64 mini (1-by-1-inch) scones

We stopped making these scones for the shops, but our customers still ask for them every single day, so I am happy to include the recipe in this book. They are loved for their size and flakiness, which can be credited to the gentle treatment of the dough. As with shortbread, we barely handle the dough, baking it while still frozen, which adds a little crispness to the flakiness. You can keep a batch of scones in the freezer to bake for weekday mornings. The crème fraîche gives a tanginess and provides an unexpected moistness. The chocolate-orange variation is a perfect winter treat.

3½ CUPS (1 POUND) ALL-PURPOSE FLOUR

½ CUP (4 OUNCES) SUGAR, PLUS EXTRA FOR SPRINKLING

½ CUP PLUS 1 TABLESPOON (4½ OUNCES) COLD UNSALTED BUTTER, DICED

2 TEASPOONS GRATED LEMON ZEST

1 TABLESPOON BAKING POWDER

¼ TEASPOON PLUS ⅛ TEASPOON BAKING SODA

1⅛ TEASPOONS SALT

⅓ CUP CRÈME FRAÎCHE (SEE NOTE)

⅓ CUP HEAVY CREAM, PLUS EXTRA FOR BRUSHING

preparation

1. In a stand mixer fitted with the paddle attachment, combine the flour, sugar, butter, lemon zest, baking powder, baking soda, and salt. Mix on low speed until the mixture resembles cornmeal. Add the crème fraîche and cream and mix until the dough is just moistened. It will look under-mixed and crumbly at this point, but it is important to stop as you will finish the mixing when you press the dough into the pan. The less you handle the dough, the flakier your scones will be.

2. In an 8-inch square baking pan, firmly press the dough as evenly as possible. Use a rolling pin to level the top if possible. The dough should be about 1 inch thick. Brush the top with cream and sprinkle lightly with sugar.

3. Mark and cut the dough into 1-inch squares. Carefully separate the cubes and put them on a parchment-lined baking sheet. Freeze for at least 1 hour, or wrap tightly and freeze up to 1 month.

4. Preheat the oven to 425 degrees F. Arrange the frozen dough squares 1½ inches apart on a parchment-lined baking sheet. Bake until the edges are toasted and golden brown, 10 to 12 minutes.

note

You can purchase crème fraîche in most gourmet grocery stores or make your own. To make it yourself, whisk together 2 cups heavy cream and 2 tablespoons buttermilk in a container. Cover and set the mixture at room temperature for 24 hours. It should become thick and tangy. Refrigerate and use as needed. It will keep for 2 weeks.

CHOCOLATE-ORANGE SCONES

Add ¼ cup (2 ounces) finely chopped candied orange and 2 ounces ground 70 percent cacao chocolate to the dough with the dry ingredients. Proceed as directed.

ÉCLAIRS

makes 16 to 18 éclairs

great !.

The éclair is one of my key barometers of a good bakery. The choux must be crisp, the pastry cream velvety, and the chocolate glaze should be more chocolatey than sweet. You can fill these éclairs with chocolate pastry cream as the French do, or plain, which is my preference. Bake your choux until it is deep golden brown and crisp so that it will stay crunchy longer. Once assembled, the éclairs will begin to get limp after a few hours, so fill them as close to serving time as possible.

½ CUP MILK

½ CUP WATER

¼ CUP PLUS 3 TABLESPOONS (3½ OUNCES) UNSALTED BUTTER

1 TABLESPOON SUGAR

1 TEASPOON KOSHER SALT

1½ CUPS (7½ OUNCES) ALL-PURPOSE FLOUR

5 LARGE EGGS, 1 WHISKED WITH 2 TABLESPOONS WATER

4 CUPS PASTRY CREAM OR CHOCOLATE PASTRY CREAM (PAGE 202)

1½ TO 2 CUPS CHOCOLATE GANACHE (PAGE 195)

preparation

1. Line two baking sheets with parchment paper. Using a pencil and ruler, lightly mark eighteen 1-by-5-inch rectangles on the parchment paper as templates for piping the éclairs. Turn the paper over and press against the bottom of the pan so you can see the lines you made. Fit a pastry bag with a medium (½- or ⅝-inch) round tip.

2. Preheat the oven to 425 degrees F.

3. In a medium saucepan, combine the milk, water, butter, sugar, and salt. Bring the mixture to a boil over medium heat.

4. Using a wooden spoon, stir in the flour and stir energetically over low heat until the dough is very thick and pulls away from the sides of the pan, about 3 minutes. Some of the moisture should evaporate.

5. Transfer the dough to the bowl of a stand mixer fitted with the paddle attachment. Beat on medium speed for 1 minute, then begin adding 4 of the eggs, one at a time. Stop and scrape down the sides of the bowl as needed. Once the eggs are all added, raise the speed to high speed and beat for 1 minute to add a little extra air to build structure.

6. Transfer some of the dough to the pastry bag fitted with a ½-inch round tip. Carefully pipe tall strips of dough to fit the templates. The strips should be about ¾ inch tall so that they rise sufficiently. When they are all piped, brush each strip with the whisked egg using a pastry brush. Gently brush the back of a fork along the dough to make grooves down the length of them. This helps them bake evenly. You can scrape up and re-pipe any mistakes, but they will not rise quite as well.

7. Bake the dough for 15 minutes without disturbing. Turn off the oven and leave the pastry inside until they are browned and feel light and hollow, 20 to 25 minutes longer. Immediately pierce each end of the pastry with the large end of a chopstick to release the steam. Transfer the pastry to wire racks and let cool completely.

8. Fit a pastry bag with a ¼-inch round tip and fill with pastry cream that has been whisked smooth. Carefully pipe pastry cream into a hole on the end of each éclair without letting it seep out, making sure there is pastry cream throughout the whole éclair.

9. Warm the ganache until it flows easily. You can add some warm water to it to thin it out. Pour the ganache into a shallow bowl. Dip the top of each filled éclair in the warm ganache, letting the excess drip off. Set the finished éclairs on wire racks to dry. Once the ganache is dry, serve the éclairs immediately or refrigerate, covered, for up to 3 hours.

candies and creams

CANDIES AND CREAMS

There is a candy and pastry shop in Vienna called Demel. It has huge windows with amazing vignettes made of cakes and candies. The downstairs is the patisserie, where you can buy cakes to take home. Upstairs is the tea salon. Along the way, you can peer into their lovely kitchen. My first trip was in 1991 and it made such a strong impression on me that when we designed our Hayes Valley candy shop, I just wanted it to be a San Francisco version of Demel.

We started making caramels the year the candy shop opened and they were so popular that we couldn't keep up with production. Next came the toffee and marshmallows, followed by the caramel corn.

Candy making requires a few specific tools. A candy thermometer in particular is essential, as most of the recipes require heating sugar and water to specific high temperatures, and several of the recipes call for tempering the chocolate, which makes it shiny and snappy. You will also need a heavy-gauge pot, thick oven mitts, and latex gloves.

You must be very careful when making candy as sugar at high temperatures is prone to sputtering, especially when you add further ingredients, and can cause serious burns. Don't let this dissuade you, just be alert. Be sure to store all candies in airtight containers to keep them crisp. Also in this chapter are our panna cotta and pots de crème, which we sell at the bakery as self-contained confections.

ENGLISH TOFFEE

makes about 3½ pounds

Miette's version of this classic candy is crisp, crunchy, and especially thin. Our English Toffee is coated in dark chocolate, then tossed in roasted almonds. Our American version uses milk chocolate and roasted peanuts. Both versions need to be stored in airtight containers.

Make sure you have a pan big enough to spread your toffee thin. A Silpat baking mat is essential to this recipe as it allows you to remove the toffee easily from the pan.

Miette's toffee is coated on both sides with chocolate and nuts. You have the option of stopping at one, but we've provided instructions for coating the second side.

ingredients

2 CUPS (9½ OUNCES) WHOLE ALMONDS (MORE IF COATING BOTH SIDES)

1 CUP (8 OUNCES) UNSALTED BUTTER

1 CUP (7 OUNCES) SUGAR

1 TABLESPOON VANILLA EXTRACT

1½ TEASPOONS SALT

⅓ CUP WATER

1½ POUNDS 70 PERCENT CACAO CHOCOLATE (MORE IF COATING BOTH SIDES)

preparation

1. Preheat the oven to 350 degrees F. Line a baking sheet with sides (a jelly-roll pan) with a silicone baking mat.

2. Toast the almonds on a second baking sheet in the oven until lightly browned, 8 to 10 minutes. Let cool and chop finely.

3. In a medium saucepan, combine the butter, sugar, vanilla, salt, and water over low to medium-low heat. Clip a candy thermometer to the side of the pan. Cook, whisking, until the butter has melted and the mixture has emulsified. Increase the heat to medium-high and cook, whisking constantly at a consistent speed, until the mixture reaches 300 degrees F, 15 to 20 minutes.

4. Pour the hot toffee onto the prepared baking sheet. Be careful as the toffee is very hot. Using an offset spatula, spread into a thin, even layer over the entire baking sheet and let cool for at least 45 minutes before adding the chocolate.

continued

5.   Meanwhile, place the chocolate in a heatproof bowl on top of a pot of simmering water and gently stir with a rubber spatula until it has melted completely, looks smooth, and is no more than 110 degrees F. Wipe off any excess oil on top with a paper towel. Spread the top of the cooled toffee with the warm chocolate and sprinkle with the nuts. Let set at room temperature until hard, 20 to 30 minutes.

6.   If desired, once the first side has set, invert the toffee onto a second sheet pan. Remove the silpat and cover the second side with additional chocoalte and nuts.

7.   Break the cooled toffee into pieces. Store in an airtight container at room temperature for up to 3 days.

AMERICAN TOFFEE

Substitute milk chocolate and lightly salted peanuts for the dark chocolate and toasted almonds. Proceed as directed.

FLEUR DE SEL CARAMELS

makes sixty-four 1-inch square caramels

Although many people feel they have to choose between a hard and soft caramel, Miette's are right in the middle. The trick to controlling the texture is in the temperature, so you must use a calibrated candy thermometer and watch it very carefully. If you let the temperature rise above 246 degrees F, the result will be a hard, chewy candy. If it doesn't reach that temperature, the caramel will be gooey and pale. We make our caramels dark and buttery with flakes of fleur de sel to finish. We also make Lemon Verbena and Chocolate variations, which are included.

Be sure to cook the caramel in a medium saucepan (at least 6 quarts), as the bubbling mixture will double in volume.

ingredients

1½ CUPS HEAVY CREAM

1¼ CUPS WHOLE MILK

2 CUPS (14 OUNCES) GRANULATED SUGAR

1¼ CUPS (8 OUNCES) LIGHT BROWN SUGAR

1 TEASPOON KOSHER SALT

2 TABLESPOONS UNSALTED BUTTER

½ CUP LIGHT CORN SYRUP

3 TABLESPOONS WATER

¼ CUP FLEUR DE SEL FOR SPRINKLING

preparation

1. Butter the bottom and sides of an 8-inch square baking dish or casserole. Line the bottom with a piece of parchment paper long enough to extend over two opposite sides by about 3 inches, to use later as handles, if needed.

2. In a medium saucepan, combine the cream, milk, granulated and brown sugars, salt, butter, corn syrup, and water. Clip a candy thermometer to the side of the pan. Place over medium-low heat and cook, whisking constantly, until the mixtures reaches 246 degrees F, 30 to 40 minutes.

3. When the caramel reaches the correct temperature, remove it from the heat and pour into the buttered pan, scraping out any caramel clinging to the sides of the pan. Be careful because the caramel is very hot. Let the caramel cool for 15 minutes and sprinkle with fleur de sel, then let

continued

STEP 2:   Cook until the mixture reaches 246 degrees F.

STEP 3:   Pour the hot caramel into the buttered pan or mold.

cool completely to room temperature. Wrap the baking dish in plastic wrap and refrigerate the whole pan for at least 30 minutes and up to 1½ hours to help it set up and make cutting the caramels easier.

4. To remove the caramel from the pan, loosen the sides by running the tip of a knife around the edges. Lift the caramel out using the parchment paper "handles." If it resists, warm the bottom of the pan briefly with a kitchen torch or over a stove burner. Turn the caramel out onto waxed paper on a cutting board. Measure 1-inch intervals along the sides, and then cut the caramel into 1-inch squares. Peel the caramel squares from the parchment paper.

5. Wrap each caramel in a square of waxed paper or candy cellophane and twist both ends. Store in an airtight container for up to 10 days.

LEMON VERBENA OR BERGAMOT CARAMELS

Stir ¼ teaspoon verbena or bergamot essential oil (see Sources, page 218) into the caramel right after you remove it from the heat. Proceed as directed, omitting the fleur de sel.

CHOCOLATE CARAMELS

Add 8 ounces finely chopped 62 percent cacao chocolate to the ingredients and cook, whisking constantly, until the mixture reaches 230 degrees F. Proceed as directed, including the fleur de sel.

Chocolate Caramels

CARAMEL CORN

makes about 10 cups

Our Ferry Building store is down the street from the Giants' stadium, and during baseball season, thousands of fans stream by on their way to a game. We thought it would be fun to reinvent the classic seventh-inning treat, so we came up with this fresh-popped Caramel Corn, topped with dark buttery caramel sauce mixed with the pivotal ingredient: Spanish peanuts. Spanish peanuts are silky and creamy while still being crunchy.

Once you pour the caramel over the corn, you need to work quickly to distribute it evenly across all the popped corn and nuts. Be careful because it is hot! You will need heat-resistant spatulas (such as silicone) to properly toss the mixture. Once it is completely cooled, store your Caramel Corn in an airtight container. At Miette, we package it in cello bags tied with ribbon.

ingredients

10 CUPS POPPED POPCORN

1 CUP (4 OUNCES) SPANISH PEANUTS, TOASTED

2 CUPS (1 POUND) FIRMLY PACKED LIGHT BROWN SUGAR

1¾ CUPS (14 OUNCES) UNSALTED BUTTER

1 CUP LIGHT CORN SYRUP

1 TEASPOON VANILLA EXTRACT

1 TEASPOON BAKING SODA

1 TEASPOON KOSHER SALT

preparation

1. Preheat the oven to 350 degrees F. Line two baking sheets with sides (jelly-roll pans) with parchment paper.

2. Divide the popcorn and peanuts between the baking sheets.

3. In a medium saucepan, combine the brown sugar, butter, and corn syrup over medium-low heat. Clip a candy thermometer to the side of the pan. Cook the mixture, whisking constantly, until it reaches 280 degrees F. Take it off the heat and stir in the vanilla, baking soda, and salt. Pour the caramel over the popcorn and peanuts, dividing it between the baking sheets. Use silicone spatulas to carefully stir the mixture to coat the popcorn and peanuts evenly.

4. Bake the popcorn and peanuts for 10 minutes. Remove the trays from the oven and stir the mixture to ensure that the caramel and peanuts are evenly distributed.

5. When fully cooled, break up the chunks of caramel corn and store in an airtight container or bags for up to 7 days.

MERINGUES

makes about sixty-five 2-inch meringues or mushrooms

Meringues are cloud-like and ephemeral in their lightness—almost like sea foam, which is a colloquial name for them.

Every bakery has extra egg whites on hand at the end of the week and you will, too, after making the recipes in this book. This is a great use for them. The key to great meringues is to dry them out slowly and completely at a low temperature, preferably in a food dehydrator. This ensures that they are meltingly crisp and light. Meringues can have infinite variations of flavor, color, and additions such as nuts, cacao nibs, and chocolate chips. Our year-round flavor is a rose geranium, which we make using essential oil from Eatwell Farms (see Sources, page 218) and tint the meringue to the palest shade of pink. At Christmas time, we flavor them with peppermint oil and call them Snowflakes. This recipe, a Swiss meringue, is also what we use to make the mushrooms for the Bûche de Noël.

ingredients

7 LARGE EGG WHITES

2 CUPS PLUS 2 TABLESPOONS (1 POUND) SUGAR

ROSE GERANIUM OR PEPPERMINT ESSENTIAL OIL (OPTIONAL)

2 DROPS RED FOOD COLORING (OPTIONAL)

1 DROP EGG YELLOW FOOD COLORING (OPTIONAL)

preparation

1. Preheat the oven to 200 degrees F. Line two baking sheets with parchment paper.

2. In a medium saucepan over medium-high heat, combine the egg whites and sugar. Clip a candy thermometer to the side of the pan. Heat the mixture, stirring to melt the sugar, until it reaches 140 degrees F. Transfer to the bowl of a stand mixer fitted with the whisk attachment. Whisk on high speed until the meringue is fluffy and has cooled to room temperature, 70 to 75 degrees F. Flavor and color it at the end by whisking in a drop or two of essential oil and the food coloring, as desired.

3. To make meringue kisses, fit a pastry bag with a medium (½- or ⅝-inch) star tip and fill it with meringue. Pull up the cuff and twist it to seal and tighten the meringue down into the cone. Purge the bag of air bubbles by squeezing the bag until there is a burst of air and meringue sputters out of the bag. Pipe 2-inch rosettes, 1 inch apart, onto the prepared baking sheets. Dry them out in the oven until crisp but not browned, 4 to 6 hours. Let cool completely, then store in an airtight container for up to 7 days.

continued

MERINGUE MUSHROOMS

To make mushrooms to decorate the Bûche de Noël (page 74) or other cakes, use a medium (½- or ⅝-inch) round tip to pipe 1-inch "stems" onto one of the prepared baking sheets and 1-inch round "caps" on the second sheet. Use a wet finger to smooth the tops of the caps before baking as directed. When the meringues have cooled completely, dust the caps and stems lightly with cocoa powder and glue them together with a dab of chocolate icing (to look like the gills) or additional meringue.

MIETTE MARSHMALLOWS

makes about forty-eight 1½-inch square marshmallows

A fresh marshmallow is a world apart from the campfire variety. The Miette marshmallow is moist, creamy, and speckled with bits of vanilla bean. We took our time developing this recipe to get the consistency just right, somewhere between fluffy and dense. We pipe our batter into cylindrical silicone molds so they resemble the jet-puffed version, but they can take any shape or form. For ease, in this recipe you smooth the confection into a pan and cut into squares. This marshmallow is most outstanding when floating in a cup of dark European-style hot chocolate.

ingredients

½ CUP (1½ OUNCES) CORNSTARCH

½ CUP (1¾ OUNCES) SIFTED POWDERED SUGAR

3 TABLESPOONS PLUS 2 TEASPOONS UNFLAVORED GELATIN POWDER (1 OUNCE OR 4 PACKETS)

⅓ CUP WATER, PLUS ½ CUP

2 CUPS (14 OUNCES) GRANULATED SUGAR

½ CUP LIGHT CORN SYRUP

½ VANILLA BEAN

3 LARGE EGG WHITES

1 TABLESPOON VANILLA EXTRACT

PINCH OF CREAM OF TARTAR

¼ TEASPOON KOSHER SALT

preparation

1. Have ready a 9-by-13-inch pan lightly coated with cooking spray. In a small bowl, stir together the cornstarch and powdered sugar. Dust the bottom and sides of the pan with the cornstarch mixture. Tap off the excess and reserve.

2. In a small bowl, sprinkle the gelatin over the surface of the ⅓ cup water. Set aside to soften.

3. In a small saucepan, combine the granulated sugar, corn syrup, and ½ cup water. Cut the vanilla bean in half lengthwise and scrape the seeds into the sugar. (Save the pod for another use.) Clip a candy thermometer to the side of the pan. Over medium-low heat, cook the mixture to 246 degrees F.

continued

4. Meanwhile, in the bowl of a stand mixer fitted with the whisk attachment, combine the egg whites, vanilla, cream of tartar, and salt. When the syrup reaches 230 degrees F, start to whisk the egg whites on low speed. When it reaches 246 degrees F, immediately remove the syrup from the heat and whisk in the softened gelatin until no lumps remain. Pour the syrup through a fine-mesh sieve into another pan or a heat-proof bowl.

5. With the mixer still on low speed, pour in a small amount of the syrup, away from the whisk so the hot syrup doesn't splash. Continue to add the syrup in a thin stream; when all of the syrup has been added, raise the speed to medium-high. Continue to whisk until the meringue has cooled to room temperature and stiff peaks form. Scrape it out into the prepared pan and smooth the top. Dust the top with some of the remaining cornstarch mixture. Cover the pan and allow the marshmallows to set for approximately 6 hours.

6. To cut, slip an offset spatula between the marshmallow and the sides of the pan. Invert the slab onto a cutting board dusted with the cornstarch mixture. Using a lightly oiled knife, cut the marshmallows into 1½-inch squares. Dust the cut edges with the cornstarch mixture and store in an airtight container or bag for up to 5 days.

CHOCOLATE POTS DE CRÈME

makes eighteen 2-ounce or nine 4-ounce pots

There is no other recipe in which I insist that you use a specific chocolate. You must use Valrhona Caraque 56%. After testing all the chocolates on the market, I found that Valrhona is the only one that doesn't leave a chalky mouth feel. This recipe is slightly tricky when it comes to determining when the pots are done. Look for a slight jiggle in the center and remove it from the oven. I have an eclectic collection of porcelain pot de crème jars that I found at flea markets. I love that they each have their own little lid, which helps in the baking and looks elegant when served. You can use ramekins or 2-ounce jars, as we do for the shops.

ingredients

7½ OUNCES 56 PERCENT CACAO CHOCOLATE OR BITTERSWEET CHOCOLATE, ROUGHLY CHOPPED

½ TEASPOON KOSHER SALT

1½ CUPS HOMOGENIZED WHOLE MILK

1½ CUPS HEAVY CREAM

GENEROUS ⅓ CUP (3 OUNCES) SUGAR

2 LARGE WHOLE EGGS

3 EGG YOLKS

WHIPPED CREAM FOR GARNISH

GRATED CHOCOLATE FOR GARNISH

preparation

1. Preheat the oven to 350 degrees F. Put the chopped chocolate and salt in a medium heatproof bowl. Set aside.

2. In a medium saucepan, combine the milk, cream, and sugar. Bring to a low boil, stirring to dissolve the sugar. Pour the hot mixture in three additions over the chocolate, stirring between each addition to combine. Let the chocolate mixture cool to room temperature, approximately 30 minutes; an instant-read thermometer should register 70 to 75 degrees F.

3. Bring a large kettle of water to a boil.

4. In a separate bowl, whisk together the eggs and egg yolks. Use a whisk or immersion blender to combine them with the cooled chocolate mixture to make a custard. Pour the custard mixture through a fine-mesh strainer into a clean 4-cup bowl with a spout, such as a large measuring cup.

5.   Divide eighteen 2-ounce jars or nine 4-ounce ramekins between two 9-by-13-inch roasting pans. Pour the custard mixture into the jars to the base of the neck or divide between the ramekins. Carefully pour hot water into the pans to reach one-third of the way up the sides of the custards. Cover each pan tightly with foil. Place each pan on an oven rack and bake for 20 minutes, then carefully open each cover (away from your face) to release some steam. Re-cover the pans and bake for another 10 minutes. Release the steam and then re-cover and bake until the custards are firm, about 20 minutes longer. (The whole process should take 35 to 40 minutes total for both sizes.)

6.   Carefully transfer the pans to a wire rack and uncover. Leave the custards in the hot water to cool for 15 or 20 minutes, then wipe each cup clean. Cover each serving with jar lids or plastic wrap and refrigerate the pots de crème until they are thoroughly cold, 2 to 3 hours. Serve garnished with a dollop of whipped cream and a grating of chocolate. These will keep in the refrigerator, covered, for up to 3 days.

BUTTERMILK PANNA COTTA

makes twelve to fourteen 2-ounce panna cottas

The tangy buttermilk and vanilla bean make this panna cotta a luscious base for any summer fruit, including strawberries, raspberries, and blueberries.

In this recipe, we use powdered gelatin. Be sure to measure the gelatin since the amounts that come in the packages will vary. Also be sure to follow the directions on the package to fully dissolve the gelatin so the dessert is smooth and properly set.

ingredients

2 CUPS HEAVY CREAM

1 TEASPOON UNFLAVORED GELATIN POWDER (ABOUT ½ PACKET)

⅓ CUP (2½ OUNCES) SUGAR

⅓ VANILLA BEAN

1 CUP PLUS 2 TABLESPOONS BUTTERMILK

FRESH BERRIES, FINELY DICED, FOR GARNISH

preparation

1. In a medium bowl, pour in ⅓ cup of the cream and scatter the gelatin evenly over the surface. Leave the gelatin to soften for at least 10 minutes. Arrange 14 clean small jars in a baking pan and clear space in your refrigerator for the pan.

2. Meanwhile, combine the remaining 1⅔ cups cream and the sugar in a medium saucepan. Split the vanilla bean lengthwise and scrape the seeds into the cream. Bring to a boil and add the dissolved gelatin mixture into the hot cream. Add the buttermilk to the cream mixture and whisk to combine. Strain the mixture through a medium-mesh strainer into a container with a spout, such as a glass measuring cup.

3. Pour the mixture into the jars just to the base of the neck. Cover the pan with plastic wrap and refrigerate overnight to set the panna cottas. Garnish with the fresh berries. These will keep in the refrigerator, covered with plastic wrap for up to 3 days; garnish just before serving.

miette essentials

MIETTE ESSENTIALS

In line with our must-have cakes, we refined our frostings and fillings to the following essentials: buttercream, cream cheese frosting, boiled icing, pastry cream, chocolate ganache, lemon curd, and variations of creamy mousse. As with all of our recipes, our fillings and frostings are about subtlety and the pure flavor that comes from using the best ingredients (especially butter) and techniques. The role of a frosting is to provide a flavor and a break in texture without overriding the cake itself. We offer a number of frostings and fillings that range in sweetness and richness and balance each of our constructed cakes.

Buttercream, in particular, is one of my passions and you will find two versions here, one made with egg yolks and one made with egg whites. Both are velvety smooth and have multiple flavor variations. The one with yolks, referred to as a French buttercream, is richer and silkier. The one with whites is lighter, holds up better to piping, and is more sturdy, which is helpful if the cake will be served outdoors. Buttercreams must be served at room temperature. By contrast, boiled icing and cream cheese frosting can be served both chilled and at room temperature.

In this chapter, you will also find recipes for sumptuous fillings, including pastry cream and chocolate ganache, two truly essential components to any bakery, as well as fruit mousses and lemon curd, which we use to bring seasonality to our cakes. Finally come the simple syrups, which add a hint of flavor and provide a little mystery.

Most of the recipes in this section yield a larger quantity than you need for a single cake. The recipes simply cannot easily be scaled down to smaller quantities. Since it is better to have too much than too little, we've provided storage instructions where possible.

VANILLA BUTTERCREAM

makes about 6 cups, enough to frost two 6-inch cakes

"Bury me in buttercream," I say, because this classic frosting is silky and luxurious and rich and light all at the same time. European butter-creams, delicious and excellent for decorating, start with a base of egg whites or yolks, whereas American-style buttercreams tend to be a sim-ple mixture of butter and powdered sugar. Granted, American butter-cream is very simple to make, but the results are lackluster at best and we don't use them at Miette. Euro-pean buttercreams provide a vastly superior texture and flavor and are worth the slightly nerve-wracking procedure.

When I teach classes, I hear more cries of panic when making butter-cream than any other task, because it is easy to "break"—that is, for it to separate into distinct masses of water and fat all of sudden—in the middle of the process. When you are making buttercream, it is important to have the ingredients at room tem-perature and to add the butter slowly so that it has a chance to become incorporated and emulsified. If your buttercream does separate, don't give up. Usually you can remedy any

continued

ingredients

2 CUPS (14 OUNCES) SUGAR

⅓ CUP WATER

5 LARGE EGG WHITES

1 TEASPOON CREAM OF TARTAR

3 CUPS (1½ POUNDS) UNSALTED BUTTER, AT ROOM TEMPERATURE

2 TABLESPOONS VANILLA EXTRACT

preparation

1. In a small saucepan over medium heat, combine the sugar and water. Clip a candy thermometer to the side of the pan. Cook the mixture until it reaches ~~248~~ *240°* degrees F, 5 to 10 minutes, keeping a constant eye on it.

2. Meanwhile, combine the egg whites and cream of tartar in the bowl of a stand mixer fitted with the whisk attachment. When the sugar syrup reaches 240 degrees F, whisk the egg whites on medium-low speed until soft peaks form. Slowly pour in the syrup, raise the speed to high, and whisk until stiff peaks form.

3. When the sugar syrup reaches ~~248~~ *240°* degrees F, reduce the speed to low and very carefully drizzle the syrup into the mixer bowl, away from the whisk so the hot syrup doesn't splatter. Be careful because the syrup is very hot. When you have added all of the syrup, raise the speed to high and beat until the mixture is cool to the touch (an instant-read thermom-eter should register 65 to 70 degrees F), 5 to 10 minutes.

continued

"disaster" by increasing the speed of your mixer or by holding a torch to the side of the bowl.

Buttercream must be served at room temperature, otherwise it is unpleasantly firm and you won't experience its luxuriousness.

Our Vanilla Buttercream is essentially a meringue buttercream made with egg whites that we then flavor to make many of our other varieties.

Vanilla Buttercream looks pure white against a dark chocolate cake and accepts additional flavors, such as fruit juices, more readily, while keeping a smooth texture. It also has significantly less fat than French Buttercream (page 188), so it is able to hold up better in heat—a consideration for an outdoor event.

4. Only when the meringue is cool enough should you begin adding the butter. Reduce the speed to medium. With the mixer running, drop in the butter, 1 tablespoon at a time, waiting until each is incorporated before adding another. The mixture may deflate and begin to look curdled. Raise the speed to high and continue to add tablespoon-size pieces of butter, making sure each is completely combined before adding more. When all of the butter has been added, the frosting should be smooth and thick. Add the vanilla and mix to combine.

5. Use the buttercream immediately, or cover and refrigerate until needed. Store in a zippered plastic bag for up to 1 week in the refrigerator and up to 2 months in the freezer. (To thaw, leave in the refrigerator overnight, not on the countertop.) To use buttercream that has been chilled, remove from the refrigerator and bring to room temperature, about 1 hour, or microwave in 15-second intervals, mixing in between each, until soft. If frosting has been frozen, this can take up to 2 minutes total. You can also soften the buttercream over a bain-marie or a double boiler. The frosting will soften from the outer edges of the bowl so mix from the outside, folding the frosting inside. Transfer to a stand mixer fitted with the paddle attachment and beat until soft and spreadable, 2 to 3 minutes.

LEMON BUTTERCREAM

For each 1 cup of Vanilla Buttercream, stir in 3 tablespoons Lemon Curd (page 200) until well combined and smooth.

PISTACHIO BUTTERCREAM

For each 1 cup of Vanilla Buttercream, stir in 2 tablespoons pistachio paste (see Sources, page 218) until well combined and smooth.

ROSE GERANIUM BUTTERCREAM

For each 1 cup of Vanilla Buttercream, stir in 2 drops rose geranium oil (see Sources, page 218) until well combined and smooth.

GRAPEFRUIT BUTTERCREAM

For each 1 cup of Vanilla Buttercream, stir in 1 tablespoon freshly squeezed grapefruit juice and 1 teaspoon grated grapefruit zest until well combined and smooth.

RASPBERRY BUTTERCREAM

For each 1 cup of Vanilla Buttercream, stir in 3 tablespoons raspberry juice until well combined and smooth. To make raspberry juice, in a saucepan over medium-low heat, combine 2 cups fresh raspberries, 2 tablespoons water, and 1 tablespoon sugar. Cook, gently stirring the berries to help them break down, until the berries are liquefied, 10 to 15 minutes. Remove from the heat and strain into a heatproof bowl through a fine-mesh sieve. Let cool to room temperature before adding to the buttercream.

FRENCH BUTTERCREAM

makes about 6 cups, enough to frost two 6-inch cakes

French buttercream is enriched with both yolks and butter and its silkiness is simply sensual. It can go on any cake, and it spreads very well and is very easy to pipe. We use this buttercream as the base for the chocolate buttercream that goes on our cupcakes in the winter months. In the summer months, the Ferry Building gets too warm and this frosting starts to melt. During that time, we substitute it with the raspberry version of our Vanilla Buttercream (page 185), whose color is so vibrant we are asked if we use red food coloring.

The mixture of egg yolks and sugar syrup in this recipe is called a *bombe* in French and is the base of almost every mousse and frosting in French baking. It is important to whisk the yolk and sugar mixture until it is completely cool; this stabilizes the *bombe* base and also prevents it from melting the butter.

Be sure to serve this buttercream at room temperature.

ingredients

1 CUP (7 OUNCES) SUGAR

½ CUP WATER

7 LARGE EGG YOLKS

2 CUPS (1 POUND) UNSALTED BUTTER, AT ROOM TEMPERATURE

preparation

1. In a small saucepan, combine the sugar and water. Clip a candy thermometer to the side of the pan and place over high heat. Bring the mixture to a rolling boil, stirring to dissolve the sugar. Cook the mixture until it reaches 238 degrees F, keeping a constant eye on it.

2. Place the egg yolks in the bowl of a stand mixer fitted with the whisk attachment. When the sugar syrup reaches 220 degrees F, begin whisking the egg yolks on medium speed. They should get frothy and lighten in color.

3. As soon as the sugar syrup reaches 238 degrees F, remove it from the heat. Pour a few tablespoons into the yolks, away from the whisk, so the hot syrup doesn't splash, and whisk on medium speed for a few seconds. Be careful as the syrup is very hot. Pour in a little more syrup and whisk for a few seconds, until incorporated. Repeat until all the syrup has been added. Raise the speed to high and whisk until the yolks thicken and turn light yellow. Continue to whisk until the mixture cools to room temperature, 70 to 75 degrees F.

4. Only when the egg mixture is cool enough should you begin adding the butter. Reduce the speed to low. With the mixer running, drop in the butter, 1 tablespoon at a time, waiting until each is incorporated before adding another. As it thickens, scrape down the sides of the bowl with a rubber spatula and continue to add the butter. When all of the butter has been added, whisk the buttercream on high speed for 30 seconds to finish it. The frosting should be smooth and thick.

5. Use the buttercream immediately, or cover and refrigerate until needed. Store in a zippered bag for up to 1 week in the refrigerator and up to 2 months in the freezer. (To thaw, leave in the refrigerator overnight, not on the countertop.) To use buttercream that has been chilled, remove from the refrigerator and bring to room temperature, about 1 hour, or microwave in 30-second increments until soft. Transfer to a stand mixer fitted with the paddle attachment and beat until soft and spreadable, 2 to 3 minutes.

CHOCOLATE BUTTERCREAM

Before beginning the buttercream, in a bowl, using an electric mixer set on high speed, beat the butter, a scant ¼ cup (2 ounces) Chocolate Ganache (page 195), and 3 tablespoons sifted natural unsweetened cocoa powder until well combined, 2 to 3 minutes. Proceed as directed, adding the chocolate-flavored butter to the yolks.

COFFEE BUTTERCREAM

Before beginning the buttercream, in a bowl, using an electric mixer set on high speed, beat the butter with 1½ tablespoons instant espresso powder until well combined, 2 to 3 minutes. Proceed as directed, adding the coffee-flavored butter to the yolks.

CREAM CHEESE FROSTING

makes about 3 cups

Tangy and sweet, classic cream cheese frosting has topped both carrot cake and gingerbread forever and far be it from us to separate these classic American pairings. Although it was difficult to improve on the original recipe, we have added a few steps to the method to keep the consistency smooth and shiny; softening the butter and creaming it with the sugar until smooth before adding the cream cheese will eliminate any little bits of butter that have a tendency to pop up in cream cheese frosting.

ingredients

2 CUPS (1 POUND) CREAM CHEESE

½ CUP PLUS 3 TABLESPOONS (5½ OUNCES) UNSALTED BUTTER, AT ROOM TEMPERATURE

1 CUP (5½ OUNCES) SIFTED POWDERED SUGAR

preparation

1. To soften the cream cheese, put it in a microwave-safe bowl and microwave on high for 10-second intervals, until completely squishy but not at all melted, stopping to check in between every interval. Set aside. (If your butter is not fully room temperature, soften the same way.)

2. In the bowl of a stand mixer fitted with the paddle attachment, combine the butter and sugar. Beat until completely smooth and glossy.

3. Add the cream cheese to the butter mixture and mix thoroughly. Use immediately or cover and refrigerate until needed. Transfer cold frosting to a stand mixer fitted with the paddle attachment and beat until smooth before using, 2 or 3 minutes. Cream cheese frosting lasts for 2 weeks in the refrigerator, tightly covered. It does not freeze.

BOILED ICING

makes about 4 cups, enough to frost two 6-inch cakes

My mother always made 7-minute icing, soft and fluffy and reminiscent of a big wedding dress. It is unapologetically sweet and miraculously light and smooth. This icing is technically an Italian meringue and it gets shinier and denser the longer you whip it, so take your time. The cream of tartar helps control the crystallization of the sugar. The temperature will mount slowly and then rapidly as it approaches the end, so keep an eye on it.

This recipe makes enough for two 6-inch cakes. Leftovers do not hold in the refrigerator as they lose volume, so serve it that day if possible. Unfortunately, we could not scale this recipe for less than 4 cups, so you will have extra if you make just one 6-inch cake.

ingredients

1½ CUPS (10½ OUNCES) SUGAR

¼ TEASPOON CREAM OF TARTAR

¼ CUP WATER

3 LARGE EGG WHITES

1 TEASPOON VANILLA EXTRACT

preparation

1. Combine the sugar, cream of tartar, and water in a small saucepan fitted with a candy thermometer. Stir the sugar to dissolve and begin to heat it over medium-low. Have a heatproof measuring cup sitting nearby.

2. Put the egg whites and vanilla in a stand mixer fitted with the whisk attachment. When the sugar syrup reaches 240 degrees F, immediately pour it into the measuring cup to prevent it from getting hotter. With the mixer on medium speed, slowly pour the sugar syrup into the egg whites, aiming for the side of the bowl rather than the whisk. When all the syrup is added, turn the mixer to medium-high and whisk until the icing becomes thick and holds a firm peak. Continue to whisk until the icing is just slightly warm and very thick, about 10 minutes total. Do not continue to beat, or the icing will become too thick to spread and pipe.

3. Use immediately on the Lime Meringue Tart (page 111), Old-Fashioned Cake (page 59), or on any other cake. Boiled icing must be used fresh and cannot be stored.

CHOCOLATE GANACHE

makes about 3 cups

We make 20 gallons of chocolate ganache every week at Miette as it is used in or on many of the things we make: as a glaze for the Bittersweet Ganache Cake (page 63) and Éclairs (page 158); as a filling for the Chocolate Truffle Tart (page 107) and our Parisian Macarons (page 145); as a frosting for the Bumblebee Cake (page 51); and swirled into French Buttercream (page 188) to make a chocolate variation.

Miette's recipe for this exquisite, velvety ganache is based on a recipe by Robert Linxe in the cookbook from La Maison du Chocolat in Paris, *La Maison du Chocolat: Transcendent Desserts by the Legendary Chocolatier*, which is why we call it the "MDC" in the bakery. We use chocolate with 62 percent cacao. Guittard and Scharffen Berger are our preferred brands, but feel free to try any chocolate to your taste.

ingredients

10 OUNCES 62 PERCENT CACAO CHOCOLATE, CHOPPED

⅔ CUP (2½ OUNCES) SIFTED POWDERED SUGAR

¾ CUP PLUS 1 TABLESPOON HEAVY CREAM

2 LARGE EGG YOLKS

3 TABLESPOONS UNSALTED BUTTER, AT ROOM TEMPERATURE

preparation

1. Combine the chocolate and powdered sugar in a heatproof bowl.

2. In a saucepan over medium heat, bring the cream to a gentle simmer. Pour the hot cream over the chocolate and stir until the sugar is dissolved. Nest the bowl over a pan of simmering water to make a bain-marie. Heat, stirring, until all of the chocolate is melted and the mixture is smooth. Remove the bowl from the heat.

3. Whisk the egg yolks in a small heatproof bowl. Pour about ½ cup of the melted chocolate mixture into the yolks while whisking, to temper them. Pour the tempered mixture back into the pan of chocolate and whisk to combine. Add the butter and stir until smooth. Pour the hot ganache through a fine-mesh sieve into a clean heatproof bowl.

4. Use the ganache immediately, or transfer to an airtight container and refrigerate for up to 2 weeks. Ganache does not freeze well.

continued

When ganache is chilled, it quickly hardens to a solid. To reheat for pouring or spreading, scoop it into a microwave-safe bowl and microwave on high for 1 minute. Next, microwave on 50 percent power for 10-second intervals, stirring between each, until the ganache reaches the desired consistency. You will usually need to add 1 or 2 tablespoons of hot water to loosen a cold ganache. For a glossy shine, it needs to return to the mixer for beating. For more specific instructions, see individual recipes.

CHOCOLATE-COFFEE GANACHE

Add 1 tablespoon plus 1 teaspoon freshly ground dark roast coffee to the cream before bringing it to a boil. Let the coffee infuse in the cream off the heat for 10 minutes, then strain out the coffee grounds through a paper coffee filter or a double thickness of cheesecloth and proceed as directed.

CHOCOLATE-HAZELNUT GANACHE

For every 1 cup Chocolate Ganache, stir in 2 tablespoons hazelnut paste (see Sources, page 218) until well combined and smooth.

CHOCOLATE-ORANGE GANACHE

For every 1 cup Chocolate Ganache, stir in 1 tablespoon orange zest and 2 tablespoons orange juice until well combined and smooth.

CHOCOLATE MOUSSE

makes about 4 cups

This chocolate mousse is very easy to make and tastes like a cup of fluffy hot chocolate. Adding the chocolate to the egg and sugar mixture while the mixer is going prevents the chocolate from seizing up and forming hard flakes in the mousse. This mousse is stabilized with sugar syrup, not gelatin. That allows the mousse to set in the refrigerator and then be used in the assembly at a later time (mousse made with gelatin requires immediate assembly). You must work quickly with this mousse once it is out of the refrigerator or it will start to melt.

Use the mousse immediately in the Bûche de Noël (page 74). This recipe will make more than you need for each cake but it is terrific in individual servings.

ingredients

⅓ CUP (2½ OUNCES) SUGAR

¼ CUP WATER

5 OUNCES 62 PERCENT CACAO CHOCOLATE

6 LARGE EGG YOLKS

1½ CUPS HEAVY CREAM

preparation

1. In a small saucepan, combine the sugar and water to make a simple syrup. Bring the mixture to a boil over high heat, 3 to 4 minutes. Set aside.

2. In a heatproof bowl over a double boiler or bain-marie, melt the chocolate over barely simmering water.

3. In a stand mixer fitted with the whisk attachment, whisk the egg yolks until lemon colored and thick. On low speed, pour the sugar syrup into the egg yolks and mix on medium-high speed until light and ribbon-y and the mixture has doubled in volume, 3 to 4 minutes. On low speed again, pour the melted chocolate into the egg mixture until combined, about 2 minutes. Scrape down the sides and bottom of the bowl by hand. Whisk until cool.

4. In another mixing bowl, whip the cream until it holds soft peaks. On low speed, slowly add the chocolate mixture to the cream. Switch to high speed and whisk until it is completely blended and holds stiff peaks. Use immediately or keep refrigerated for up to 3 days, tightly sealed. Freeze in a tightly sealed container for up to 2 months.

STRAWBERRY MOUSSE

makes about 4 cups

We recommend you make this luscious mousse in the late spring or early summer when strawberries are at their peak at your local farmers' market. Make this recipe the day you plan to make your cake as it sets up right away. This recipe makes more than you will need for the Strawberry Charlotte (page 45), but the extra makes a delicious dessert on its own either poured into a bowl or into individual ramekins, topped with whipped cream.

ingredients

5 CUPS (25 OUNCES) STRAWBERRIES, HULLED AND QUARTERED

⅓ CUP (2½ OUNCES) SUGAR

½ TEASPOON FRESHLY SQUEEZED LEMON JUICE

2 TABLESPOONS WATER

2 TEASPOONS UNFLAVORED GELATIN POWDER

¾ CUP HEAVY CREAM

preparation

1. In a small saucepan over very low heat, cook the strawberries, sugar, lemon juice, and water until very liquid, about 30 minutes. Strain the mixture through a sieve and let cool completely. You should have 1¼ cups of strawberry juice.

2. Pour ¾ cup of the juice into a small bowl and sprinkle the gelatin over the surface to soften.

3. Reheat the remaining juice until it is warm to the touch. Add the softened gelatin mixture to the warm juice and whisk until the gelatin has completely dissolved.

4. In a stand mixer with the whisk attachment, whip the cream until it holds medium peaks. Fold one-third of it into the strawberry mixture. Gently fold in the remaining whipped cream until no streaks remain.

5. Pour the mousse into a bowl (or ramekins) and store in the refrigerator for up to 3 days.

COCONUT MOUSSE

makes about 4 cups

Coconut is pure and distinct in this mousse, which itself is light and creamy. You must use fresh coconut purée to achieve this flavor—anything else imparts an artificial or suntan-lotion taste. We buy our purée from Perfect Purées of Napa Valley (see Sources, page 218), which is the only place we have been able to source a product that has the right sweetness and texture. Once the mousse is set, you cannot reuse it. So, when making the Coconut Mousse Cake (page 41), it is important to have your other components ready for assembly before you start the mousse procedure.

(page 218)
(page 41)

ingredients

1½ CUPS (13 OUNCES) COCONUT PURÉE

2 TEASPOONS UNFLAVORED GELATIN POWDER

¼ CUP (2 OUNCES) SUGAR

1 CUP HEAVY CREAM

preparation

1. Pour ¾ cup of the purée into a small bowl and sprinkle the gelatin over the surface to soften.

2. In a small saucepan, heat the remaining purée and the sugar over low heat until the sugar dissolves. Stir the softened gelatin mixture into the warm purée and stir to dissolve the gelatin. If lumps remain, put the pan over low heat and stir just until the lumps dissolve. Pour the mixture through a fine-mesh strainer into a large bowl. Let the mixture cool to room temperature.

3. In a stand mixer fitted with the whisk attachment, whip the cream until it holds medium peaks. Fold one-third of it into the coconut mixture. Fold in the remaining whipped cream until no streaks remain.

4. Pour the mousse into a bowl (or ramekins) and store in the refrigerator for up to 3 days.

LEMON CURD

makes about 2 cups

The most difficult thing about lemon curd is determining when to take the mixture off the bain-marie. The cooking term is *nappé*, which means that if you stick a wooden spoon in the curd, run your finger through the coating on the back of the spoon, and get a trail that sticks, the curd is done. Once you take the curd off the bain-marie, let it cool for about 20 minutes before adding the butter. Adding the butter at this point is what makes a truly great curd as the cooler temperature allows butter to maintain its supple creamy qualities since it is not fully melted. Use the freshest eggs possible because a vibrant yolk will impart the most beautiful golden tone.

ingredients

1 CUP (7 OUNCES) SUGAR

½ CUP FRESHLY SQUEEZED LEMON JUICE

1 TABLESPOON LEMON ZEST

7 LARGE EGG YOLKS

½ CUP (4 OUNCES) UNSALTED BUTTER, CUBED

preparation

1. In a heatproof bowl, whisk together the sugar, lemon juice, lemon zest, and egg yolks. Set the bowl over a pot of simmering water to make a bain-marie. Whisking occasionally, cook the mixture until it thickens considerably (to about 172 degrees F).

2. Remove from the heat and strain through a fine-mesh sieve into a clean container. Let the curd cool slightly (to about 140 degrees F), for approximately 20 minutes.

3. Using an immersion blender or a whisk, mix the butter into the curd until the butter is completely incorporated. Strain again to remove any lumps. Place plastic wrap directly on the surface of the curd to prevent a skin from forming and refrigerate until well chilled before using to assemble tarts, cakes, or other pastries. Lemon curd will keep for up to 7 days tightly covered in the refrigerator. It also freezes beautifully for up to 3 months.

PASTRY CREAM

makes about 2½ cups

very thin
did not thicken up

My favorite pastries are those with custard, especially when it is rich and supple. Pastry cream is an essential but subtle component in our Éclairs (page 158), in the Princess Cake (page 34), and in our Pastry Cream and Fresh Fruit Tart (page 115). Texture defines a good pastry cream; it needs to be smooth as silk and just thick enough to hold its shape without becoming rubbery. The key to achieving this is to cook off the cornstarch, as uncooked cornstarch feels chalky in your mouth. Using only egg yolks heightens the flavor and gives the cream a lovely pale yellow hue. If you have time, allow the vanilla beans to steep in your milk for an hour before proceeding with the rest of the recipe. Pastry Cream does not store well in the freezer.

ingredients

2 CUPS WHOLE MILK

½ VANILLA BEAN

7 LARGE EGG YOLKS

½ CUP (3½ OUNCES) SUGAR

2 TABLESPOONS CORNSTARCH

2 TABLESPOONS UNSALTED BUTTER, AT ROOM TEMPERATURE

preparation

1. Pour the milk into a medium pot. Use a sharp knife to slit the vanilla bean lengthwise and scrape the seeds into the milk. Put the pod in the milk as well. Heat the milk until almost boiling (bubbles will begin to form at the edges). Cover and let steep for 1 hour if time permits, otherwise proceed as directed.

2. In a medium bowl, whisk together the egg yolks, sugar, and cornstarch until smooth. Set the bowl on a kitchen towel or nonskid surface and whisk the egg mixture while pouring about ½ cup of the hot milk into the mixture to temper. Gradually pour in the rest of the milk, whisking constantly. Pour the contents of the bowl into the pan and set over medium-low heat.

3.	Cook, whisking constantly, until the mixture thickens and comes to a slow boil, about 2 minutes. Immediately strain the cream through a fine-mesh sieve into a clean container. Discard the vanilla bean or wash and reuse it. Let the pastry cream cool to room temperature, 10 minutes, and then whisk in the butter. You want the butter to be incorporated without being melted.

4.	Cover the pastry cream with plastic wrap, pressing the plastic directly on the surface of the cream to prevent a skin from forming. Refrigerate until well chilled, at least 1 hour and up to 3 days.

CHOCOLATE PASTRY CREAM

Warm 2 tablespoons Chocolate Ganache (page 195) for every 1 cup Pastry Cream. Stir them together until incorporated. Refrigerate until fully cool.

LADYFINGERS

makes two 3-by-10-inch bands, more than enough to encircle a 6-inch cake

Despite their romantic name, lady-fingers are mostly utilitarian. They are basically a sponge cake that can be piped and syruped in countless variations. For our purposes, this recipe creates two bands of con-nected cookies to surround and support the Strawberry Charlotte (page 45). The ladyfingers need to be piped right next to each other so that when they bake, they will rise up and touch each other. You will need parchment paper for this recipe, so you can draw a template on the opposite side to guide you in your piping. The powdered sugar dusted on the ladyfingers before they go into the oven gives them a powdery patina.

For the Charlotte cake, you will need a 19-inch band, but cookie sheets are only 14 inches so we've directed you to pipe out two bands that add up to slightly more than you will need. You will have to trim them to fit.

ingredients

1 CUP (5 OUNCES) ALL-PURPOSE FLOUR

5 LARGE EGGS, SEPARATED, PLUS 2 LARGE EGG WHITES

¾ CUP (5½ OUNCES) GRANULATED SUGAR

POWDERED SUGAR FOR DUSTING

preparation

1. Line a large baking sheet with parchment paper. Using a pencil, draw two 3-by-10-inch rectangular templates on the paper, one above the other. Turn the paper over and press against the bottom of the pan so you can see the pencil lines you made.

2. Fit a pastry bag with a medium (½- or ⅝-inch) round tip. Sift the flour into a bowl and set aside.

3. In the bowl of a stand mixer fitted with the whisk attachment, beat the egg yolks with 2 tablespoons of the granulated sugar on medium-high speed until thick and ribbony. Scrape the mixture into a wide bowl and set aside.

4. Clean the bowl and the whisk. Combine the egg whites and the remain-ing granulated sugar in the bowl and whisk on high speed until stiff peaks form. Fold the whites into the yolks in three additions, just until no streaks remain.

5. Sift about one-third of the flour over the egg mixture and fold in gently. Fold in the remaining flour in two more additions, until just combined. Fill the pastry bag with the batter. Starting ¼ inch from a short end of the first template, pipe each finger, ¾ inch by 3 inches, down the length of each template, using the lines to guide you and placing them next to each other so that the fingers join together when they bake. (You should have 10 fingers for each band.) Using a fine-mesh sieve, dust the tops of the piped batter with the powdered sugar. Let the unbaked cookies stand at room temperature for 15 minutes.

6. Preheat the oven to 350 degrees F.

7. Dust the ladyfingers again with powdered sugar and bake until just beginning to turn golden, 8 to 10 minutes. Transfer to wire racks to cool. As soon as they are just barely cool, use immediately or wrap in plastic wrap, being careful not to let the bands break apart, so that they don't dry out. Store in airtight containers for up to 2 days.

SIMPLE SYRUP

makes 1 cup

We use our simple syrups to infuse our cakes with flavor and add a little moisture. Simple syrups add a subtle background note to our Lemon Debutante Cake (page 29), Princess Cake (page 34), Bumblebee Cake (page 51), and Lemon Tea Cake (page 92). You only need a few tablespoons per cake, but since simple syrups can be stored for up to a month, it's convenient to make a cup or two and use as needed.

ingredients

1 CUP (7 OUNCES) SUGAR
1 CUP WATER

preparation

In a small saucepan, combine the sugar and water and bring to a boil over medium-high heat, stirring to dissolve the sugar. When the sugar is completely dissolved and the syrup is clear, remove from the heat and let cool to room temperature. The simple syrup will keep, tightly sealed in the refrigerator, for up to 1 month.

LEMON SIMPLE SYRUP

In a small saucepan, combine ½ cup water, ¼ cup fresh lemon juice, and ¼ cup sugar and bring to a boil over medium-high heat, stirring to dissolve the sugar. Let cool and store tightly sealed in the refrigerator for up to 1 month. Makes ¾ cup.

RASPBERRY SIMPLE SYRUP

Stir 1 teaspoon raspberry eau-de-vie (see Sources, page 218) into ¼ cup Simple Syrup.

COCONUT SIMPLE SYRUP

Stir ½ cup coconut milk (see Sources, page 218) into ½ cup Simple Syrup. Store tightly sealed in the refrigerator for up to 1 month.

essential ingredients
and
essential tools

ESSENTIAL INGREDIENTS

Sourcing local, organic ingredients was quite a challenge when I started the bakery a decade ago—flour, chocolate, and sugar produced this way were difficult to find. As the local, organic movements have grown, more and more shelves are filled with carefully crafted choices. Although we still have to make trade-offs based on what is available, we are constantly in pursuit of the best local, chemical-free, and sustainable products. This commitment has paid off, as we have developed wonderful relationships with farmers and vendors whose quality products make ours infinitely better.

Here are guidelines for the essential ingredients we use at Miette, including some of both our local sources and widely available go-to brands. To achieve the distinctive flavors and textures that only organic ingredients can provide, use the best local and/or organic products you can find. Of course, many good-quality ingredients can be purchased online as well.

CHOCOLATE AND COCOA POWDER

The recipes in this book were originally designed around Scharffen Berger cocoa and chocolate with their fruity, bright taste profiles. I met co-founder Robert Steinberg at the farmers' market and we spent hours talking about chocolate. Since then, we've experimented with other chocolates ranging from 56 to 70 percent.

chocolate

We use 56 percent, 62 percent, and 70 percent cacao in the bakery. Variations in chocolate come mainly from the inherent flavor of the bean and the ratio of sugar, milk, and cocoa.

I like bright, crisp almost fruity chocolate flavor with about 70 percent cacao. This gives depth and flavor to cakes. In our Chocolate Buttercream (page 189), we use a combination of melted chocolate and cocoa powder to deliver a rich taste. Read the ingredients on packages and look for a product that is simple and pure—no additives, extra oils, or fillers. From there, you can experiment with different brands and percentages.

cocoa powder

It seems natural to think that the darker the cocoa powder, the more intense the flavor. This is not true. Dutch-processed cocoa has been treated with an alkalizing agent that heightens the color but gives it a milder flavor compared to natural cocoa powder. Since the two forms of cocoa will react differently with leaveners, it's wise to use a non-Dutch-processed product labeled "natural," such as Scharffen Berger, when making our recipes. We also use a brut cocoa powder, which is extra dark.

COCONUT:

coconut puree

It took us long a time to source the perfect puree and, coincidentally, it is from a company called Perfect Puree. It is unsweetened coconut cream with pectin and of very high quality (see Sources, page 218).

dried shredded coconut

We use sweetened on the outside of our coconut cake; and unsweetened goes inside our carrot cake.

DAIRY

We source all of our butter, cream, and milk from the dairy at Straus Family Creamery, a local operation in Marshall, California that is committed to the strictest production standards. They were the first organic dairy west of the Mississippi River and continue to blaze the trail in areas like non-GMO feeds, the use of recycled glass rather than plastics, and the humane treatment of their herds. Its products, richer in fat and flavor, are superior and that quality translates to the quality of our products. Sourcing fresh, local dairy ingredients will have the greatest impact on the flavor and quality of your baking, and we urge you to find a local dairy near you that carries premium products. Two good purveyors we know of are Ronnybrook and Vermont Butter & Cheese.

butter

Great-quality organic butter is truly the backbone of the bakery. Butters vary in terms of butterfat content (butter guidelines dictate at least 80 percent fat), but generally European butters have more fat. Our rule is to use the butter with the most fat, to give the best mouthfeel. Finally, always use unsalted butter. This allows more flexibility to increase or decrease the level of salt in the final product.

buttermilk

We use buttermilk any time we want a moist, somewhat dense texture with a tangy background flavor, such as in chocolate cake and pound cakes. Buttermilk is one of those flavors that is as comforting as it is exciting.

cream

Cream must be of the highest quality. We use flash-pasteurized cream from Straus Family Creamery. Conventionally pasteurized cream is taken past a certain temperature beyond a certain time limit, lessening its flavor. Dairies such as Straus have found a way to flash-pasteurize the cream for a fraction of the time and the flavor is superior. Look to your own local dairy for cream that has been flash-pasteurized.

eggs

Truly fresh, truly free-range eggs have very dark yolks, which add a gorgeous tone to lemon curd and make cakes electric yellow. For best results, find farm-fresh eggs—we use the large size—and let them come just to room temperature before using.

milk

We always use organic whole milk. Two-percent milk is fine, but nonfat milk lacks the taste and richness that benefit baking. At Miette, we use a brand of organic whole milk which is not homogenized, so the cream rises to the top. We just give the jug a vigorous shake and proceed with the recipe. One exception is our Chocolate Pots de Crème (page 178), which calls for homogenized milk, as non-homogenized milk causes the pudding to separate while baking.

FLOUR AND STARCH

To make lighter cakes, we use a mixture of all-purpose flour and potato starch. Many bakers advocate using bleached flour, but we don't like using such a highly processed product.

flour

All of the recipes in this book use all-purpose white flour. We use a locally milled organic flour with protein of 9 percent from Giusto's in the San Francisco Bay Area, but any all-purpose flour will work. All-purpose flour gives body to cakes, making them moist and delicious, whereas cake and pastry flours are flavorless and have no character.

potato starch

Potato starch provides structure and lightness in cakes without adding gluten. When used in the correct proportion with all-purpose flour, it creates our version of cake flour. This yields a lighter, silkier crumb and makes way for the use of organic sugar, which can make the cake a bit denser and not as moist. Potato starch is available in the kosher section of most grocers.

NUTS

Since our first shop was in a seventy-five-year-old nut mill, we took advantage of our facility to experiment with nuts—especially almonds, which we now use at the rate of 100 pounds a week for our macarons. Keep nuts in zippered plastic freezer bags in the freezer at all times; they tend to turn rancid very quickly at room temperature, and they need little to no thawing before using in baking (and just a few minutes to eat out of hand).

almonds

Traditional macarons use almonds that have the hull taken off and are ground to a fine powder, but we use the skin-on form, which gives our macarons a distinctive appearance and texture (you can see the specks of husk). Get the freshest unprocessed raw almonds you can find; in California, where the number-one crop is almonds, we get them directly from the farmer. If you need ground almonds, we recommend buying them already ground, but if you are grinding them yourself, use a food processor or a coffee mill. A tablespoon of cornstarch will prevent the nuts from clumping.

hazelnuts

We use organic hazelnuts in our hazelnut macarons. Grind the nuts into a coarse powder or flour using a food processor. Do not over-grind or they will turn into an unusable paste.

peanuts

Use Spanish peanuts with their skins intact. Grown primarily in Oklahoma and Texas in the United States, Spanish peanuts have a higher oil content than other types of peanuts, which makes them smoother on the tongue.

pecans

We use organic pecan halves. Toasting is essential to bring out their flavor. Place in a dry frying pan and toast over medium heat, stirring constantly, until fragrant and lightly browned, about 5 minutes. Transfer immediately to a plate to cool; nuts can burn easily.

pistachios

Use preground pistachios, if available. Otherwise, grind the nuts into a coarse powder or flour using a pulsing motion in a food processor. Do not overgrind or they will turn into an unusable oily paste.

walnuts

We generally use medium-size pieces. Toasting is essential to bring out their flavor. Place in a dry frying pan and toast over medium heat, stirring constantly, until fragrant and lightly browned, about 5 minutes. Transfer immediately to a plate to cool; nuts can burn easily.

SALT

Our recipes call for kosher salt, meaning it is unprocessed and additive free. Look for Diamond A Crystal kosher salt. This salt dissolves quickly. For the recipes in this book that highlight salt, such as the Walnut Shortbread Cookies (page 138) and Fleur de Sel Caramels (page 167), use sea salt such as coarse fleur de sel or Maldon, characterized by big flakes with a really nice flavor.

SWEETENERS

If there is any baking discovery we'd like to contribute to the pastry world, it's how to make classic cakes using organic sugar. We were the first bakery in the country to use organic sugar and develop fine pastries that could accommodate the coarse crystals of that form. This has been a key achievement on our mission to source all organic ingredients. We've included other sweeteners in this list, as well as tips for how we use them in our recipes.

honey

We like to use organic honey, and prefer its subtle floral flavors for our pastries. If you can, use honey from local hives.

light corn syrup

Corn syrup is highly processed and we avoid it whenever possible. It is, however, an essential ingredient in candy-making due to its ability to prevent the crystallization of sugar.

molasses

Since we use organic sugar, which already contains some molasses, we usually use a regular molasses.

sugar, brown

Traditional brown sugar is sugar that hasn't had the molasses taken out of it. Nowadays, most brown sugar is white sugar to which molasses has been added. Typically, light brown sugar contains 3 percent molasses and dark brown contains 6 percent molasses. At Miette, we use light brown sugar as it delivers the right amount of molasses for our taste.

sugar, granulated organic

Organic sugar comes in the form of coarse crystals made from evaporated cane juice. Because of its flavor and texture, using organic sugar can be problematic; it can make things heavy and collapse and does not give as fine a texture as white sugar. Our recipes have been calibrated to make pastries that share the same results as their highly refined cousins. If you can't find organic sugar, you can use granulated, or white, sugar in the recipes.

sugar, powdered

In the bakery, we refer to powdered, or confectioners', sugar as "10-X," because it is sugar that has been ground down to one-tenth its "normal size." Organic powdered sugar is very hard to find and is an unattractive gray color, so we use conventional powdered sugar when called for in recipes.

ESSENTIAL TOOLS

As noted throughout the book, having the right tools and equipment is essential to effective baking. Below is what we consider indispensable for the baker's kitchen.

bain-marie or double boiler

Sometimes you need to heat something gently over indirect heat to prevent scorching and burning. *Bain-marie*, or "hot water" bath, is the term for both the technique and the piece of equipment used specifically in this instance. A double boiler is essentially the same thing: a heatproof top pan that nests on top of another pan filled with simmering water. When using a bain-marie or a double boiler, you want to make sure that the simmering water does not touch the top pan or bowl.

brushes

The most useful baking brush is 1 inch wide and made with long, flexible natural bristles. Some brushes are equipped with a hook on the handle to clamp onto the side of a bowl. You should have two brushes, one for applying syrups and one to brush away crumbs. Keep these brushes exclusively for sweets—you don't want to flavor your cake with garlic butter.

cake board

You need to decide how you want to present your cake before decorating. Once frosted, it becomes very difficult, often nearly impossible, to move without putting a dent in its perfection. Cake boards, simple panels of sturdy corrugated cardboard covered with a smooth finish, offer a convenient and inexpensive solution. Setting up your cake for assembly and decoration on a board affords you a base that works like handles when you need to move the cake from a revolving work stand to the refrigerator or a cake plate or presentation platter for serving.

Cake boards are available at cake supply stores in white, silver, and gold and in a variety of shapes and sizes common to the world of cakes. They can also be trimmed to fit shaped pans or odd sizes. Typically, you need a board that is 2 inches bigger in diameter than the size of your cake pan, to allow room for frosting and any edge piping. At Miette, we created a custom-made cake board that is 8 inches in diameter, perfect for our cakes (and available to buy at our Web site).

To prevent the board from slipping on the cake stand while you work, put a nonslip pad or a folded damp paper towel beneath it. If you are concerned about what the board will do to the aesthetics of your plate, there are versions with pretty scalloped edges or even the look of lace that are "made to show," as well as coated cake boards that are easy to clean with a damp cloth before presenting.

If you don't have a cake board, or you prefer the clean look of a cake seated seamlessly on the plate, you can decorate the cake directly on its presentation plate or platter—just make sure the plate is perfectly flat (a curve can ruin the lines of the finished cake). You will also have to be prepared to take some pains cleaning up if the plate gets dirty while you work (see also Cake Stand, Revolving, page 216).

cake rack

This is necessary for properly cooling cakes. Not only does a wire cake rack provide circulation, it lets the cakes cool without them sticking to the counter. Get three or four racks for good measure.

cake stand, revolving

Essentially just a footed cake stand with a top that rotates, like a turntable or lazy Susan, the revolving cake stand is an American invention; they are unheard of in Europe, and every French intern we host takes one home with him. I find them so handy, I can barely decorate a cake without one anymore. I believe acquiring a revolving stand leads to quickly excelling in decorating, and I call for it in the recipes in this book. If you don't like the idea of working on a cake board (see page 215) and stand and then moving the cake to a serving plate, as a kind of compromise, there are revolving cake stands that are table ready—that is, pretty enough to serve from—if that suits you.

double boiler

See Bain-marie or Double Boiler.

fine-meshed sieve

You can never sieve enough: Our motto is "strain, strain, strain." We sieve everything, from fruit juices to flour. Sieving your mixtures makes them smooth and elegant, making your pastries more smooth and refined. We also use it as a post-mixing technique to ensure that we don't overmix our batters.

food processor

Essential for grinding nuts without turning them to butter. Clean thoroughly between uses.

immersion blender

Immersion blenders are good for mixing small amounts of ingredients that need to be emulsified and are indispensable for creating shine in ganache.

knife, serrated

A serrated knife is essential for cutting layers in cakes. You want the blade to be longer than the diameter of the cake: For a 6-inch cake, the knife should have an 8- or 10-inch blade.

microwave

A microwave is the best way to melt chocolate and is instrumental in heating frosting to the right temperature.

mixer, stand

A heavy-duty stand mixer, also called an upright mixer, is essential for making the recipes in this book. We recommend the KitchenAid brand, with a 5-quart bowl and whisk and paddle attachments. (Although a hand-held mixer is an alternative if you do not have access to a stand mixer, we do not recommend using one for pastries.)

pans, cake

To make a true Miette cake, we suggest you invest in specific cake pans. Miette cakes are designed using 6-by-3-inch baking pans. The smaller pan is one of the elements that define the Miette aesthetic. We also use 6-inch contour pans, which have a rounded bottom. Look for them online.

pan, cupcake

The recipes in this book are for a standard twelve-cup, 2½-inch cupcake pan.

pans, jelly-roll and baking sheet

The recipes in this book were tested using a standard low-sided jelly-roll pan for sheet cakes and a standard baking sheet for cookies and meringues.

pans, loaf

The recipes in this book call for a charmingly petite 3-by-5-inch pan, or standard 5-by-9-inch loaf pans. Find mini loaf pans in the size that suits you in kitchen-supply stores and online (see Sources, page 218).

pans, tart

The recipes here call for a 7-inch tart ring with a removable bottom pan, or 3½-inch tartlet pans. We use both fluted and straight-sided tart rings. The tart recipes have been tested for 8-inch pans as well.

pastry bag

A pastry bag is essential for laying down ingredients and for piping borders. It gives you control, and keeps your hands clean, and its precision gives the mark of a professional—once you start using pastry bags, you will want to pipe everything. We like disposable pastry bags because they are easy to use and spare you the cleanup; regular pastry bags are very hard to clean and can take on permanent odors.

piping tips

To make the recipes in this book, you will need both a small (¼- or ⅜-inch) and a medium (½- or ⅝-inch) round (also called plain, or open) tip, and small and medium star tips. Just as you'd guess, round tips have a circular opening with smooth edges and a star tip is beveled into a star shape to make pretty raised edges. Most manufacturers use a non-ruler-based numbering system to indicate size, and many of the most common tips get a number that is universal across brands. For example, our favorite tip for everyday use is the versatile Ateco #8, a medium, or ⅝-inch, round tip.

scraper

A bowl scraper is the tool found in every baker's pocket. It's easier to maneuver than a spatula.

spackle blade

A spackle blade, found at any paint or hardware store, is an essential tool for refining a cake's final frosting layer. Look for one with a 4-inch blade.

spatula

To make the recipes in this book, you will need a number of different spatulas: a rubber spatula for scraping down the sides of mixing bowls, turning out batter, and gentle folding-in of ingredients; a large, wide metal spatula for lifting up cake layers and for moving a cake from one platter to another; and an offset (icing) spatula for assembling the cakes. A heatproof or silicone spatula is useful for tossing candy corn.

thermometers

Nearly every recipe in this book calls for specific temperatures. In most cases, a candy thermometer will suffice. A candy thermometer gives the temperature in degrees and also clearly denotes critical candy temperature stages: soft ball, firm ball, hard ball. We recommend one that can clip to the side of your pot to protect your hands and help you get an accurate read. Make sure that the bottom of the thermometer meets the ingredients that you are reading; in some cases, you will need to transfer the mixture to a smaller pot to increase the depth of what you're measuring. This will retard the heating process, which can be surprisingly rapid. An oven thermometer is also very useful to confirm that your baking temperature is accurate.

SOURCES

Farmers' Markets
www.ams.usda.gov/farmersmarkets
There is no better place than local farmers' markets and farm stands to gather the best produce of the season at peak ripeness. Ask your farmers what varieties they recommend, whether it is a new type of berry for a tart or which pumpkin will make a great purée. Often you can find organic milk, butter, and cheese at the farmers' market, as well as eggs and nuts.

Albert Uster Imports
(800) 231-8154
www.auiswiss.com
A great source for specialty pastry-making ingredients, including fondant and nut pastes.

Dean & Deluca
(800) 221-7714
www.deandeluca.com
Essential oils and nut pastes, full-fat European butters, fine chocolates, organic sugars and flours, and baking equipment.

Eatwell Farms
(866) 627-2465
www.eatwell.com
Our source for essential oils.

JB Prince
(800) 473-0577
www.jbprince.com
An excellent selection of baking equipment, including contour cake pans.

KitchenAid
(800) 541-6390
www.kitchenaid.com
Heavy-duty stand mixers and other kitchen equipment.

Michael's Art Supply
(800) 642-4325
www.michaels.com
Cake boards, pastry bags and tips, and other cake-decorating supplies.

Miette
(415) 837-0300
www.miette.com
We sell 7-, 8-, and 9-inch scalloped cake boards, candied daisies, and our signature candied roses.

The Perfect Purée of Napa Valley
(800) 556-3703
www.perfectpuree.com
Pure fruit purées and juices with no added sugar; our source for coconut purée.

St. George Spirits
(510) 769-1601
www.stgeorgespirits.com
Beautiful quality spirits, including raspberry eau-de-vie.

Straus Family Creamery
(707) 776-2887
www.strausfamilycreamery.com
Our source for butter, cream, and milk.

Sur la Table
(800) 243-0852
www.surlatable.com
All manner of cooking equipment, including baking pans, tart pans, silicone molds, and Silpat mats.

Whole Foods Market
www.wholefoodsmarket.com
Whole Foods carries organic staples, including flours, sugars, eggs, milk, nut pastes, and produce.

Wholesale Sugar Flowers
(800) 593-8250
www.discountsugarflowers.com
Candied roses and daisies and other lovely flower confections.

Williams-Sonoma
(800) 541-2233
www.williams-sonoma.com
An exhaustive inventory of kitchen equipment from tools to vessels to appliances, in both classic and innovative lines.

Wilton Industries
(800) 794-5866
www.wilton.com
Baking specialist Wilton Industries is a purveyor of a seemingly infinite arsenal of baking pans, boards, and papers; pastry bags and tips; tools and cutters; decorating supplies; specialty ingredients; and more.

INDEX